Training course to increase your reading speed and study skills by

Follow the course and:

SPEED READ

- Increase your reading speed by 50 - 300%,
- Improve your comprehension and what you remember

SKIM / AUTOSKIM

- Learn techniques to rapidly get the main ideas in a document

BE MORE PRODUCTIVE IN STUDY AND WORK

- Study better - Special section on efficient study
- Increase your reading speed so you can breeze through documents
- Set-up your computer screen to read long documents faster (and go home from work early!)

FOCUS AND CONCENTRATION

- Use the techniques in this course to improve your concentration and focus.

HAVE MORE FUN AND LESS STRESS READING

If you can get through a book in a day you are more likely to read it and enjoy it.

"THE COVERS OF THIS BOOK ARE TOO FAR APART."

Ambrose Bierce, genius in need of ReadPal's Speed Reading Course

First published by Cucoco Ltd., 2005.
Unit 4, Campus Innovation Centre, National University of Ireland-Galway, Ireland.

Written by Dr Louis Crowe and Michael FitzGerald

ISBN :   1-905459-05-X

www.readpal.com Visit ReadPal for further information on Speed Reading and Speed Reading software.

Dedication

To my mother and my darling nieces and nephew, Nuanna, Andreea and Louis. May they be always happy and know the joys of reading. (And to Karen S. whom I promised to dedicate a book to 10 years ago).

I would like to specially thank...

Cathal O' Keffee, Ciaran Byrne, Claire Cullinane, Goska FitzGerald and Marcel for their honest advice and corrections.

Contents

Part I, Introduction and Preparation

Chapter 1	Overview of course	5
Chapter 2	Getting the most out of your course	9
Chapter 3	What they didn't teach you in school...	11
Chapter 4	How Speed Reading works	13

Part II, Learning to Speed Read

Chapter 5	Assessing your Baseline Reading Speed	16
Chapter 6	Preparing for the Training Sessions	25
Chapter 7	Speed Training Exercises on Printed Material	28
Chapter 8	Using your computer to Speed Train	66

Part III, Skimming and AutoSkim™

Chapter 9	Overview and Skimming	73
Chapter 10	An exercise in the Unimportance of Words	75

Part IV, Study

Chapter 11	Speed Reading and Study	99

Part V, Wrap up

Chapter 12	Consolidating your gains	107
Appendix	Graph your reading speed	111

PART I

INTRODUCTION AND PREPARATION

This section will give you an introduction to the course; answer common questions; explain what speed reading is and how it works.

It will tell you what improvements you can expect from the course and what preparation and commitment are required in order to permanently improve you reading ability.

CHAPTER 1

OVERVIEW OF THE COURSE

The course has a simple structure.

Part I of this book will give you the background to speed reading and the techniques used to improve your reading speeds. It will explain common bad habits in reading and how to overcome them. It explains how speed reading works and why.

In Part II you get your baseline reading speed (so you'll be able to quantify your improvements). You will then be given the exercises to improve your reading. Some exercises are on printed material, both in this book and on newspapers, etc. Other exercises are computer based. You will be shown how to set up your computer so that you can do special speed-training exercises.

Part III deals with effective skimming techniques.

Part IV is dedicated to improving your study skills and in particular the role of reading during your study.

Part V discusses how you should consolidate your improvements so you can always read faster.
Typically the course is completed in a month. However, the user should continue to practice to consolidate their gains. The user should regularly assess their speed in order to monitor their progress.

Like in many things in life...the more you put in the more you get out.

SOME COMMON QUESTIONS ABOUT THE SPEED READING COURSE

Question: What improvements can I expect in my reading?

Answer: You can expect big improvements. Both in your reading of printed material and in your on-screen reading. Let's talk about your print-reading first.

Typically users will increase their reading speed by 50-300%. The improvement you achieve depends on many things. Your initial reading speed, how often you train, etc. Even a 50% increase would make a huge difference to most people's lives. (50% is a lot... would you like a 50% pay increase?). A history student could expect to go up a grade with less work. A business man might have a chance of keeping up to date in his field. You might finish the Sunday papers on Sunday!

On the internet there are many who will claim to guarantee reading speeds of tens of thousands of words per minute. Whilst an occasional individual may reach such speeds and be able to remember something of what they read they really are one-in-a-million. They usually perform a type of skimming which is similar to glossing over an article. The targets we set out are achievable and you can start to benefit from the very first session.

In addition to your ability to read faster you will develop greater understanding at any given speed. You will learn to vary your reading speed to suit the subject matter.

Fun! Reading should be fun and being a better reader will help you to enjoy your reading more. If you read a book in a day or two instead of a few weeks you'll find it more absorbing.

On-screen reading, (Computer Reading).
On-screen reading tends to be slower than print-reading. The reason is that documents are often formatted to be good when printed out. However, this is usually unsuited to fast, comfortable on-screen reading.

You will be shown how to optimize the formatting for on-screen reading. This will enable you to get through very long documents and e-books with greater ease and speed.

Question: I'm a really bad reader - can it still help me?

Answer: One of the real joys of being bad at something is that there is so much room for improvement and usually big improvements are easily achieved! Consider an unfit person and an elite athlete starting on a training program for one month. The elite athlete would be lucky to improve by 1% but the unfit person could easily improve their fitness levels by 50%. So be happy if you are now a bad reader because that will soon change.

Question: If I have been reading for most of my life why do I need a course in reading?

Answer: If your reading speed is over 800 words per minute you are already in the top 1% of readers. However, you can still improve. Top readers read at *double* this speed. You can achieve these levels through persistent practice. In addition, the very fast reader finds that they can have difficulty reading rapidly on-screen because the way text is presented. By using the tricks described here or the ReadPal software they can fly through their on-screen reading.

"MEN OF POWER HAVE NO TIME TO READ; YET THE MEN WHO DO NOT READ ARE UNFIT FOR POWER."
Michael Foot

If you are already a good or very good reader you should do more than one training session in one sitting, as they'll take you less time.

Question: I am almost too busy to do the course... any suggestions?

Answer: Yes, several.

Firstly, you can train on documents that you have to read anyway, so less time will be 'lost'.

Secondly, the sessions are designed to take less than a half hour, not a lot considering the benefits of faster reading.

Lastly, calculate the number of hours you spend reading every year and see how much time you would save if you doubled your reading speed.

Question: I may read something more quickly but will I understand it and remember it as well?

Answer: Yes!

During the course you will read at speeds that are difficult for you. During some training sessions you may not understand and remember much. This is part of the training. However, when not training your reading speed will be much higher with no loss of understanding. Indeed, many, especially previously slow readers, greatly increase their understanding at all speeds. (This is probably because they no longer read single words in isolation but rather groups of words which together make the context clearer).

Question: How often should I train?

Answer: We recommend that you train for about a half an hour five times a week for a month.

THE MORE THAT YOU READ,
THE MORE THINGS YOU WILL KNOW.
THE MORE THAT YOU LEARN,
THE MORE PLACES YOU'LL GO.
Dr. Seuss

Glossary

On-screen reading   Reading on your computer screen; any digital reading.

Print / printed material reading   Reading anything 'physical', like a book, magazine or newspaper.

Words per minute / wpm   This is your reading speed. The number of words can you read in a minute with good understanding.

CHAPTER 2

GETTING THE MOST OUT OF YOUR COURSE

The course is only of use if people use it! This chapter is about how to ensure you will reap the full benefits... not just for a day, but for the rest of your life. As in much of life... you get out what you put in.

Reading is a most important skill; it deserves some time and commitment. Not much time, mind you, and not much commitment -just a little perseverance. View the time you spend speed training as an investment. Just doubling your reading speed could save you thousands of hours over the years.

Psychologists have studied why some people keep resolutions, (like New Years Resolutions), and why some don't. If you adhere to the following simple procedure you are twice as likely to succeed. By writing down a specific goal and exactly how you are going to get there the mind suddenly takes this promise more seriously. *DON'T JUST THINK IT - INK IT!* The mind finds it easy to squirm out of resolutions if they are vague, or never ending, or *too* big.

"IF YOU AIM AT NOTHING, YOU'LL HIT IT EVERY TIME."
Anonymous

The research tells us to be:

- **SPECIFIC**, (nothing vague or 'airy fairy', like "I'll improve soon"!)
- **CLEAR**
- **GOAL ORIENTED**

Remember, a promise written down is worth ten made in the mind. Writing it makes it concrete.

Things are much easier to stick with if they become habits. It is much easier if something becomes a routine. This is one reason why most people don't forget to brush their teeth. (They always do it last thing before getting into bed when they are in the bathroom). So you should try to get into the habit of doing your training at the same time everyday. You can, of course, train more than once a day, but if you promised to do it at a particular time try to keep that promise...and anything else is a bonus.

Have a look at the declaration form below. You will be asked to fill it out before you are start the speed training sessions.

"IN LIFE, AS IN FOOTBALL, YOU WON'T GET FAR UNLESS YOU KNOW WHERE THE GOALPOSTS ARE"
Arnold H. Glasgow

My Promise to Myself

I, ..., solemnly undertake to improve my reading speed.

My baseline speed is ...., this will improve by AT LEAST 50% to ......or more. (Fill this in after the first reading assessment).

I will do this by doing (tick):

☐   30 Speed Training Sessions.
☐   The printed material exercises, described in this book
☐   The exercises in this book

I will do .... number of sessions per day, (weekday). This means that I will do ..... sessions per week.

If at all possible I will do this
....
....
(E.g. every weekday first thing at work after switching on my computer - try and be specific with your time and place this help enormously- then stick with it).

Improving my reading speed will help me:
1..
2..
(Again, be specific, e.g. this will help me increase my History grade by ...).

CHAPTER 3

WHAT THEY DIDN'T TEACH YOU IN SCHOOL...

This chapter describes some common bad habits of average readers and how they can be overcome.

THREE READING HABITS OF THE AVERAGE READER.

The following are typical traits that hold people back when they are reading. We learn them in childhood and often never get rid of them:

1. Excessive sub-vocalisation
2. Back-tracking
3. Reading at the same speed

1. Excessive Sub-vocalisation

Sub-vocalisation is the term for talking under your breath or saying each word as you read it, even in your head. When we learnt to read we pronounced each letter to form a word. Then we pronounced each word. This is a good and necessary stage for learning. However, for some people, this can become a drag on speed if they insist on placing emphasis on 'hearing' each word as they read it.

Saying the words, per se, is not a problem. Many people can talk faster than most can read. Racing commentators are notorious! There are recordings of people speaking distinctly at 1,000 words per minute – five times the speed of comfortable reading for most. As you progress in speed, however, moving of the lips and hearing the words becomes less pronounced and for many stops altogether. Let this happen naturally and do not try to hear each word.

2. Back-tracking

Unnecessary back-tracking is a bad habit that is common in average readers. Average readers tend to read a few words and then go back and reread some of them. This is usually a subconscious habit - people don't even realise that they are doing it. (However, if we track a person's eye movements with a high-speed camera it is clear that they are frequently back-tracking). Most of the time this is not just unnecessary but actually hinders the understanding of the text because it becomes disjointed. Again, this is a habit we formed while learning to read. Starting out we were naturally unsure of every word we read and frequently went back to double-check that we had got it right. This is appropriate for beginners. However, if you can read this book, frequent backtracking is not appropriate for you... you've progressed well beyond that level and it is only holding you back.

You can't expect to make much progress if for every two steps forward you take one step back. It is a habit that needs to be broken. Thankfully help is at hand! The exercises in this book will help eliminate *unnecessary* backtracking. During the speed training sessions you are forced onto the next word/group of words. Backtracking regularly, (many times within a sentence), is not an option.

3. Always reading at the same speed

If you are jogging and come to a hill you will slow down because it is more difficult; you'll naturally speed up going downhill. Likewise with reading; if you are reading something difficult it is often necessary to slow down. On the other hand if you are reading something you find easy let your reading speed soar. Don't be stuck in the one gear for all your reading. Shift it around a little.

"ONCE WE HAVE LEARNED TO READ, THE MEANING OF WORDS CAN SOMEHOW REGISTER WITHOUT CONSCIOUSNESS."

Anthony Marcel

CHAPTER 4

HOW SPEED READING WORKS

This chapter describes the theory of speed reading training. Why you must push yourself to your limits and beyond. Why, like physical fitness, you must *use it or lose it*.

It is easy!

Reading is a skill and a habit. In many ways it is like physical exercise. If we never had to run we would be quite happy walking and we'd never learn how to run. Running is a different skill to walking. It is not just walking faster, the knees rise, etc. The habits of walking must be broken in order to run. As a child, when we first run we're hesitant and unsteady. With practice we get better. Likewise with speed-reading ... you must break some of the habits from your childhood ... (such as backtracking).

As with physical exercise you must push yourself to improve. It is by reaching beyond your 'comfort level' that you attain speeds you never thought were possible. If you want to run faster you must train at fast speeds. Walking a marathon won't help a sprinter much. In training if you want to sprint you must do strength and speed exercises. If you are happy reading at say 200 words per minute well and good. However, if you want to comfortably read at 600 words per minute you must train at high speeds. Speeds that initially push you and challenge you. *But persevere! Great speed comes to those who practice at great speed.*

"Use it or lose it". The fit person must regularly exercise if they want to maintain their fitness. Reading fitness must also be maintained by regularly reading at top speeds. This keeps the mind agile and prevents you from slipping back into older, slower ways.

"Time management is life management. Everybody manages time. It's not optional. Some people just do it better than others."

Dr Gene Griessman, in *How To Get More Out Of Every Day*

The eye movements during reading

When you read something the eye does not move smoothly over the text as you would imagine. Instead the eye hops along the line(s). Next time you are beside someone reading look at their eyes and your will see them jerking. The eye stops, focuses on a few letters or words, takes them in and then moves on to the next group of letters or words, focusing on them, taking them in. At each stop it takes in some information. The brain pieces all this together and you understand what has been written.

From this you can see that there are two principle ways to improve your reading speed. The first is the time spent on each focus. If you half the time per focus, (and you read the same amount with each focus), then you double the speed that you are reading at. Secondly, if you double the amount that you can read with each focus then you also increase your speed. The exercises and speed sessions train you to both increase the speed of each focus and how much you can take in with each focus.

"I HAD JUST TAKEN TO READING. I HAD JUST DISCOVERED THE ART OF LEAVING MY BODY TO SIT IMPASSIVE IN A CRUMPLED UP ATTITUDE IN A CHAIR OR SOFA, WHILE I WANDERED OVER THE HILLS AND FAR AWAY IN NOVEL COMPANY AND NEW SCENES... MY WORLD BEGAN TO EXPAND VERY RAPIDLY ... THE READING HABIT HAD GOT ME SECURELY".

H. G. Wells

Part II

Learning to Speed Read

... what they didn't teach you at school

The fun begins now ... learning how to speed read. At the end of this section you will have all the knowledge and techniques needed to increase your reading speed.

You'll check your baseline reading speeds so you can quantify your improvements.

You will be given power exercises to do on printed material. We'll also describe how computers may be used in accelerating your reading and give you exercises to do on your computer. Do these and you will begin to see results almost immediately.

Enjoy!

Chapter 5

Assessing your Baseline Reading Speed

It is good to measure how by much your reading speed is improving.

Getting your baseline reading speeds.

It is not absolutely necessary to know what your reading speed is. If you just do the training sessions you will still notice a big improvement in your reading speed. However, it is very beneficial to know it. You can quantify the improvements and set targets. This is a great motivator. You should get your baseline reading speed and then check it once every one to two weeks.

Your reading speed is defined as your ability to read X number of words per minute at reasonable comprehension and retention. We say you can read at X wpm, (words per minute).

During the Speed Assessments you should read at *a brisk but comfortable speed*. At the end of the assessment you should write down a quick, (2 minute) summary of the story. If you cannot do this you were probably reading beyond your present limits. Choose another story and repeat the assessment.

Your reading speed differs when you are reading on-screen or printed material. So to assess your *change* in reading speed you must compare like with like; using material of similar difficulty level, ideally by the same author. For most people it is best to print out the assessments.

We've chosen a Mark Twain story to start with. You will be able to find more Mark Twain stories for free download at www.readpal.com or www.gutenberg.org (Project Gutenberg is a non-profit organisation that makes books available for free).

The story is 2,149 words long.

If you are an average reader this will take you about 10 minutes, (at 215 words per minute).

1. Make sure you're in a place without too many distractions and where you won't be disturbed.

2. You'll need to time yourself how long it will take.
    You can use a stopwatch, (or the computer clock; double-click on it and it should show the seconds as well; wait for a nice round number, like five minutes past five and zero seconds, write it down if you'll forget).

3. Time how long it takes you reading at a **normal but brisk** pace such that you can understand everything.

4. Write down how long it took you.

5. Then write a brief, (1-2 minute summary) of what happened in the chapter. If you cannot write a good summary of what happened you were probably reading too quickly to catch it all. No worries...choose another story and try again.

*"Knowledge is
free at the
library. Just
bring your own
container."*
Anonymous

Assessment 1: Baseline reading-speed

A BURLESQUE BIOGRAPHY

By

Mark Twain

2,149 words

Two or three persons having at different times intimated that if I would write an autobiography they would read it when they got leisure, I yield at last to this frenzied public demand and herewith tender my history.

Ours is a noble house, and stretches a long way back into antiquity. The earliest ancestor the Twains have any record of was a friend of the family by the name of Higgins. This was in the eleventh century, when our people were living in Aberdeen, county of Cork, England. Why it is that our long line has ever since borne the maternal name (except when one of them now and then took a playful refuge in an alias to avert foolishness), instead of Higgins, is a mystery which none of us has ever felt much desire to stir. It is a kind of vague, pretty romance, and we leave it alone. All the old families do that way.

Arthour Twain was a man of considerable note--a solicitor on the highway in William Rufus's time. At about the age of thirty he went to one of those fine old English places of resort called Newgate, to see about something, and never returned again. While there he died suddenly.

Augustus Twain seems to have made something of a stir about the year 1160. He was as full of fun as he could be, and used to take his old saber and sharpen it up, and get in a convenient place on a dark night, and stick it through people as they went by, to see them jump. He was a born humorist. But he got to going too far with it; and the first time he was found stripping one of these parties, the authorities removed one end of him, and put it up on a nice high place on Temple Bar, where it could contemplate the people and have a good time. He never liked any situation so much or stuck to it so long.

Then for the next two hundred years the family tree shows a succession of soldiers--noble, high-spirited fellows, who always went into battle singing, right behind the army, and always went out a-whooping, right ahead of it.

This is a scathing rebuke to old dead Froissart's poor witticism that our family tree never had but one limb to it, and that that one stuck out at right angles, and bore fruit winter and summer.

Early in the fifteenth century we have Beau Twain, called "the Scholar." He wrote a beautiful, beautiful hand. And he could imitate anybody's hand so closely that it was enough to make a person laugh his head off to see it. He had infinite sport with his talent. But by and by he took a contract to break stone for a road, and the roughness of the work spoiled his hand. Still, he enjoyed life all the time he was in the stone business, which, with inconsiderable intervals, was some forty-two years. In fact, he died in harness. During all those long years he gave such satisfaction that he never was through with one contract a week till the government gave him another. He was a perfect pet. And he was always a favorite with his fellow-artists, and was a conspicuous member of their benevolent secret society, called the Chain Gang. He always wore his hair short, had a preference for striped clothes, and died lamented by the government. He was a sore loss to his country. For he was so regular.

Some years later we have the illustrious John Morgan Twain. He came over to this country with Columbus in 1492 as a passenger. He appears to have been of a crusty, uncomfortable disposition. He complained of the food all the way over, and was always threatening to go ashore unless there was a change. He wanted fresh shad. Hardly a day passed over his head that he did not go idling about the ship with his nose in the air, sneering about the commander, and saying he did not believe Columbus knew where he was going to or had ever been there before. The memorable cry of "Land ho!" thrilled every heart in the ship but his. He gazed awhile through a piece of smoked glass at the pencilled line lying on the distant water, and then said: "Land be hanged--it's a raft!"

When this questionable passenger came on board the ship, he brought nothing with him but an old newspaper containing a handkerchief marked "B. G.," one cotton sock marked "L. W. C.," one woollen one marked "D. F.," and a night-shirt marked "O. M. R." And yet during the voyage he worried more about his "trunk," and gave himself more airs about it, than all the rest of the passengers put together. If the ship was "down by the head," and would not steer, he would go and move his "trunk" further aft, and then watch the effect. If the ship was "by the stern," he would suggest to Columbus to detail some men to "shift that baggage." In storms he had to be gagged, because his wailings about his "trunk" made it impossible for the men to hear the orders. The man does not appear to have been openly charged with any gravely unbecoming thing, but it is noted in the ship's log as a "curious circumstance" that albeit he brought his baggage on board the ship in a newspaper, he took it ashore in four trunks, a queensware crate, and a couple of champagne baskets. But when he came back insinuating, in an insolent, swaggering way, that some of this things were missing, and was going to search the other passengers' baggage, it was too much, and they threw him overboard. They watched long and wonderingly for him to come up, but not even a bubble rose on the quietly ebbing tide. But while every one was most absorbed in gazing over the side, and the interest was momentarily increasing, it was observed with consternation that the vessel was adrift and the anchor-cable hanging limp from the bow. Then in the ship's dimmed and ancient log we find this quaint note:

"In time it was discouvered yt ye troublesome passenger hadde gone downe and got ye anchor, and toke ye same and solde it to ye dam sauvages from ye interior, saying yt he hadde founde it, ye sonne of a ghun!"

Yet this ancestor had good and noble instincts, and it is with pride that we call to mind the fact that he was the first white person who ever interested himself in the work of elevating and civilizing our Indians. He built a commodious jail and put up a gallows, and to his dying day he claimed with satisfaction that he had had a more restraining and elevating influence on the Indians than any other reformer that ever labored among them. At this point the chronicle becomes less frank and chatty, and closes abruptly by saying that the old voyager went to see his gallows perform on the first white man ever hanged in America, and while there received injuries which terminated in his death.

The great-grandson of the "Reformer" flourished in sixteen hundred and something, and was known in our annals as "the old Admiral," though in history he had other titles. He was long in command of fleets of swift vessels, well armed and manned, and did great service in hurrying up merchantmen. Vessels which he followed and kept his eagle eye on, always made good fair time across the ocean. But if a ship still loitered in spite of all he could do, his indignation would grow till he could contain himself no longer --and then he would take that ship home where he lived and keep it there carefully, expecting the owners to come for it, but they never did. And he would try to get the idleness and sloth out of the sailors of that ship by compelling them to take invigorating exercise and a bath. He called it "walking a plank." All the pupils liked it. At any rate, they never found any fault with it after trying it. When the owners were late coming for their ships, the Admiral always burned them, so that the insurance money should not be lost. At last this fine old tar was cut down in the fullness of his years and honors. And to her dying day, his poor heart-broken widow believed that if he had been cut down fifteen minutes sooner he might have been resuscitated.

Charles Henry Twain lived during the latter part of the seventeenth century, and was a zealous and distinguished missionary. He converted sixteen thousand South Sea islanders, and taught them that a dog-tooth necklace and a pair of spectacles was not enough clothing to come to divine service in. His poor flock loved him very, very dearly; and when his funeral was over, they got up in a body (and came out of the restaurant) with tears in their eyes, and saying, one to another, that he was a good tender missionary, and they wished they had some more of him.

Pah-go-to-wah-wah-pukketekeewis (Mighty-Hunter-with-a-Hog-Eye-Twain) adorned the middle of the eighteenth century, and aided General Braddock with all his heart to resist the oppressor Washington. It was this ancestor who fired seventeen times at our Washington from behind a tree. So far the beautiful romantic narrative in the moral story-books is correct; but when that narrative goes on to say that at the seventeenth round the awe-stricken savage said solemnly that that man was being reserved by the Great Spirit for some mighty mission, and he dared not lift his sacrilegious rifle against him again, the narrative seriously impairs the integrity of history. What he did say was:

"It ain't no (hic) no use. 'At man's so drunk he can't stan' still long enough for a man to hit him. I (hic) I can't 'ford to fool away any more am'nition on him."

That was why he stopped at the seventeenth round, and it was a good, plain, matter-of-fact reason, too, and one that easily commends itself to us by the eloquent, persuasive flavor of probability there is about it.

I also enjoyed the story-book narrative, but I felt a marring misgiving that every Indian at Braddock's Defeat who fired at a soldier a couple of times (two easily grows to seventeen in a century), and missed him, jumped to the conclusion that the Great Spirit was reserving that soldier for some grand mission; and so I somehow feared that the only reason why Washington's case is remembered and the others forgotten is, that in his the prophecy came true, and in that of the others it didn't. There are not books enough on earth to contain the record of the prophecies Indians and other unauthorized parties have made; but one may carry in his overcoat pockets the record of all the prophecies that have been fulfilled.

I will remark here, in passing, that certain ancestors of mine are so thoroughly well-known in history by their aliases, that I have not felt it to be worth while to dwell upon them, or even mention them in the order of their birth. Among these may be mentioned Richard Brinsley Twain, alias Guy Fawkes; John Wentworth Twain, alias

Sixteen-String Jack; William Hogarth Twain, alias Jack Sheppard; Ananias Twain, alias Baron Munchausen; John George Twain, alias Captain Kydd; and then there are George Francis Twain, Tom Pepper, Nebuchadnezzar, and Baalam's Ass--they all belong to our family, but to a branch of it somewhat distinctly removed from the honorable direct line--in fact, a collateral branch, whose members chiefly differ from the ancient stock in that, in order to acquire the notoriety we have always yearned and hungered for, they have got into a low way of going to jail instead of getting hanged.

It is not well, when writing an autobiography, to follow your ancestry down too close to your own time--it is safest to speak only vaguely of your great-grandfather, and then skip from there to yourself, which I now do.

I was born without teeth--and there Richard III had the advantage of me; but I was born without a humpback, likewise, and there I had the advantage of him. My parents were neither very poor nor conspicuously honest.

But now a thought occurs to me. My own history would really seem so tame contrasted with that of my ancestors, that it is simply wisdom to leave it unwritten until I am hanged. If some other biographies I have read had stopped with the ancestry until a like event occurred, it would have been a felicitous thing for the reading public. How does it strike you?

STOP the watch!

Assessment 1. Baseline reading speed for printed material.

Time taken to read *A BURLESQUE BIOGRAPHY*: _____

Next write a brief summary of the story:

_____

_____

_____

_____

_____

_____

_____

_____

_____

_____

_____

_____

_____

_____

_____

_____

_____

_____

_____

_____

_____

_____

_____

_____

_____

_____

_____

_____

_____

_____

_____

_____

_____

_____

_____

_____

Ideally you should calculate the exact words per minute.   Or as an approximation use the following:

The story has 2,149 words so if you read it in....

40 minutes your reading speed is 54 words per minute.
30 minutes your reading speed is 72 wpm.
20 minutes your reading speed is 107 wpm.
17 minutes your reading speed is 126 wpm.
15 minutes your reading speed is 143 wpm.
13 minutes your reading speed is 165 wpm.
12 minutes your reading speed is ~~279~~ wpm. *179 wpm*
11 minutes your reading speed is ~~295~~ wpm. *195 wpm*
10 minutes your reading speed is 214 wpm.
9 minutes your reading speed is 239 wpm.
8 minutes your reading speed is 269 wpm.
7 minutes your reading speed is 307 wpm.
6 minutes your reading speed is 358 wpm.
5 minutes your reading speed is 429 wpm.
4 minutes your reading speed is 537 wpm.
3 minutes your reading speed is 716 wpm.
2 minutes your reading speed is 1,075 wpm.
1 minute your reading speed is 2,149 wpm.

You should write down your reading speed and keep it so you can track your progress. This is best done by marking it on the graph at the end of this book. (It is very satisfying to see your speed go up).

WELL DONE! You've taken the first few steps to becoming a better, faster and more efficient reader.

You should assess and graph your reading speed once a week until you have completed the course.

"A JOURNEY OF A THOUSAND MILES BEGINS WITH A SINGLE STEP".

– Proverb

Chapter 6

Preparing for the Training Sessions

This chapter will give information on the training sessions - what they are like and how you should prepare for them.

There are 4 types of speed training exercises; two are on printed material and two are computer based.

Printed-material exercises:

Exercise 1.   A speed boosting exercise.
Exercise 2.   Visual-Span Exercise. Designed to expand your visual span, (how many words you can focus on at a glance).

Computer-based training exercises

Exercise 3.   A speed boosting exercise on your computer.
Exercise 4.   Visual-Span Exercise. The computer based system is very effective.

(There are two further exercises to help you practice the art of skimming).

Material for the Speed Training Sessions

With the exception of the visual span exercises you can choose what material to do your speed session on. It should not be too technical, heavy or have lots of graphs or tables.

A suitable collection of free material is to be found at the free downloads section and the speed section of ReadPal, www.readpal.com. You can use a short story for each session. They are a selection of wonderful but simple stories, written by some of the world's greatest authors. The authors include James Joyce, Mark Twain, and Leo Tolstoy...

"OUTSIDE OF A DOG, A BOOK IS A MAN'S BEST FRIEND.
INSIDE OF A DOG, IT'S TOO DARK TO READ."
Groucho Marx

Preparing for a session.

An athlete needs to be prepared to get the most out of their training, so do you...

Where you read is important. Set aside the time, (about a half-hour), in a place where you won't be disturbed.

Reading position and posture.

This is important for two reasons. Firstly, a good reading posture will help your concentration. If you are slumped in your chair or reclining on your couch you won't get the full benefit from the session. Secondly for your general health. If, like many of us, you're sitting all day long a bad posture can do great harm.

Make sure that you are sitting comfortably. Do not strain to get into a position... if it is a strain on your body it is probably doing harm. Your feet should be flat on the floor; your back should be supported and your bum pushed well into the chair. (This will help keep your back straight and aligned).

The following are indicators of good reading posture.

- The book should be on a table or flat surface
- Arms resting on the table
- Ears, shoulders and hips aligned
- Bum well tucked into seat and lower back supported
- Knees at or slightly below hip level, (i.e. use a high chair)
- Legs uncrossed
- Feet flat or on rest

In addition, for good on-screen reading posture:

- Eyes level with the monitor - consider raising the monitor

Before starting you should take a couple of deep breaths to help release any tension.

"THIS NOVEL IS NOT TO BE TOSSED LIGHTLY ASIDE,
BUT HURLED WITH GREAT FORCE."
Dorothy Parker

Poor Posture

Good Posture - note the alignment of ear, shoulder and hip.

Chapter 7

Speed Training Exercises on printed material

You are thaught how to pace your reading. Then there are two exercises on printed material. The first is a simple speed exercise where you read at an increasing pace. The second is designed to increase your visual span.

Before you start: learn this technique to pace your reading

There is a simple but remarkable exercise for reading on printed material. Use a finger or a pen as a pacer to keep your reading speed up. This seems too simple to be effective... but once you have tried it you will be convinced. You set your pen or finger at a fast speed and your eyes try to keep up. It has the added benefit of making it easier for your eyes to focus as they have a point of reference.

The most convenient pacer to use is your index finger. Children often use their finger to guide where their eye should read. There is much merit in this, (despite many a teacher banning it!). Pacing with a finger is only a sign of poor or slow reading when the finger is moving slowly or backtracking. If the finger is moving quickly it clearly indicates the opposite, i.e. a confident, proficient and fast reader.

As you get faster the finger / pen movement changes. Initially, you should move the tip rapidly under the line that you wish to read. Then move onto the next line. The eyes move following the pacer. Practice doing this at increasing speeds.

Level 1. The line represents the movement of your pen or index finger. It runs along the line of text you are reading (red) then hops over onto the next line (black).

As you progress, or force greater speeds, you'll find that your movements become less completed. Your finger or pen does not finish the full width of each line. As you go to greater speeds again it becomes a broad zigzag down the page. Even though your pacer does not point to every word you still read every word. This is because the pointer is used as a reference point for eyes to focus and a pacer.

Level 2. At faster speeds the lines become less complete until it is just a broad sweep down the page.

Level 3, the pacer moves straight down the page or column

With greater practice and speed you can move onto moving the pointer straight down the page. Of course, only very proficient readers can hope to take in a line or more of text in a single focus. Most people take in each line first with a focus to the left of the pacer then to the right. This is done at a subconscious level. You don't need to be aware of your eye movements. You only need to force the pace - your eyes will take care of the rest.

This straight-down movement is ideal for high-speed practice and, in particular, for reading newspapers and text in columns. Many newspapers print at least some of their paper in columns of five or six words each. It is an *achievable* objective to sweep straight down a narrow newspaper column taking in one line with each focus / fixation.

You can convert most computer documents into a narrow column format with a large font size to practice. You can print these out or read them on-screen. However, you must use your pacer. For on-screen reading you can still use your finger if you find controlling the mouse awkward. You should resolve to use a pacer for all your reading for the next six weeks. For this period *always* read at the limit of your abilities until what were once fantastic speeds become the norm for you.

Exercise 1. General Speed Training

Get easy reading material, then using your finger or pen to pace:

1   Read at your maximum speed (for good comprehension) for 5 minutes. Note how far you have read.
2   Reread to the same spot in 4 minutes.
3   Reread to the same spot in 3 minutes.
4   Reread to the same spot in 2 minutes.

You should practice this everyday for 2 weeks and thereafter weekly.

"A ROOM WITHOUT BOOKS IS LIKE A BODY
WITHOUT A SOUL."

Marcus T. Cicero

Exercise 2. Increasing your Visual Span

As previously discussed, your reading speed is approximately the number of words that you can take in one focus multiplied by the number of focuses per minute. For most people there seems to be an optimal number of focuses per minute, (about 150-250 or ~3-4 frames per second). Reading speed is generally improved by reading at the optimal number of focuses per minute and increasing what can be taken in in a focus, i.e. you read more with each focus.

Below is *The Legend of Sleepy Hollow*, by Washington Irving. It is divided into columns, like a newspaper. Initially there is only one word per line. You should take each line of a column in with **one** focus. The words per line are gradually increased until there are five or six words per line - this is the width of a narrow newspaper column.

Continue to try to take each line in with just **one** focus as the number of words per line increases. (You should continue to do this even if you begin to lose the sense of what is being said, remember this is an exercise to increase your focus. You may need to reread it several times to understand it).

Many readers will be able to focus on more than one word at a time. However, they should still go through the exercise from the start. Firstly, as it is a beautifully written story. Secondly, because it gets you comfortable in reading one line at a time and establishes a rhythm for this type of reading. You should try and keep moving down the columns just as fast when it goes from one word per column to two.

This exercise is about 50 standard pages long so you may like to do it in more than one session. If you are doing the exercise properly it will take you less than an hour. If you are breaking it up it is an idea to reread what went before at two or three times your normal speed.

"EVERYWHERE I GO, I'M ASKED IF THE UNIVERSITIES STIFLE WRITERS. MY OPINION IS THAT THEY DON'T STIFLE ENOUGH OF THEM."

Flannery O'Connor

THE LEGEND OF SLEEPY HOLLOW

By

Washington Irving

In
the
bosom
of
one
of
those
spacious
coves
which
indent
the
eastern
shore
of
the
Hudson,
at
that
broad
expansion
of
the
river
denominated
by
the
ancient
Dutch
navigators
the
Tappan
Zee,
and
where
they
always
prudently
shortened
sail
and
implored
the
protection
of
St.
Nicholas
when
they
crossed,
there
lies
a
small
market
town
or
rural
port,
which
by
some
is
called
Greensburgh,
but
which
is
more
generally
and
properly
known
by
the
name
of
Tarry
Town.

This
name
was
given,
we
are
told,
in
former
days,
by
the
good
housewives
of
the
adjacent
country,
from
the
inveterate
propensity
of
their
husbands
to
linger
about
the
village
tavern
on
market
days.

Be
that
as
it
may,
I
do
not
vouch
for
the
fact,
but
merely
advert
to
it,
for
the
sake
of
being
precise
and
authentic.

Not
far
from

this
village,
perhaps
about
two
miles,
there
is
a
little
valley
or
rather
lap
of
land
among
high
hills,
which
is
one
of
the
quietest
places
in
the
whole
world.

A
small
brook
glides
through
it,
with
just
murmur
enough
to
lull
one
to
repose;
and
the

occasional
whistle
of
a
quail
or
tapping
of
a
woodpecker
is
almost
the
only
sound
that
ever
breaks
in
upon
the
uniform
tranquility.

I
recollect
that,
when
a
stripling,
my
first
exploit
in
squirrel-
shooting
was
in
a
grove
of
tall
walnut-trees
that
shades
one
side
of

the
valley.

I
had
wandered
into
it
at
noontime,
when
all
nature
is
peculiarly
quiet,
and
was
startled
by
the
roar
of
my
own
gun,
as
it
broke
the
Sabbath
stillness
around
and
was
prolonged
and
reverberated
by
the
angry
echoes.

If
ever
I
should
wish

for
a
retreat
whither
I
might
steal
from
the
world
and
its
distractions,
and
dream
quietly
away
the
remnant
of
a
troubled
life,
I
know
of
none
more
promising
than
this
little
valley.

From
the
listless
repose
of
the
place,
and
the
peculiar
character
of
its
inhabitants,

who to Master subject
are pervade Hendrick to
descendants the Hudson. trances
from very and
the atmosphere. Certain visions,
original it and
Dutch Some is, frequently
settlers, say the see
this that place strange
sequestered the still sights,
glen place continues and
has was under hear
long bewitched the music
been by sway and
known a of voices
by High some in
the German witching the
name doctor, power, air.
of during that
SLEEPY the holds The
HOLLOW, early a whole
and days spell neighborhood
its of over abounds
rustic the the with
lads settlement; minds local
are others, of tales,
called that the haunted
the an good spots,
Sleepy old people, and
Hollow Indian causing twilight
Boys chief, them superstitions;
throughout the to stars
all prophet walk shoot
the or in and
neighboring wizard a meteors
country. of continual glare
his reverie. oftener
A tribe, across
drowsy, held They the
dreamy his are valley
influence powwows given than
seems there to in
to before all any
hang the kinds other
over country of part
the was marvelous of
land, discovered beliefs, the
and by are country,

and
the
nightmare,
with
her
whole
ninefold,
seems
to
make
it
the
favorite
scene
of
her
gambols.

The
dominant
spirit,
however,
that
haunts
this
enchanted
region,
and
seems
to
be
commander-in-
chief
of
all
the
powers
of
the
air,
is
the
apparition
of
a
figure
on
horseback,

without
a
head.

It
is
said
by
some
to
be
the
ghost
of
a
Hessian
trooper,
whose
head
had
been
carried
away
by
a
cannon-ball,
in
some
nameless
battle
during
the
Revolutionary
War,
and
who
is
ever
and
anon
seen
by
the
country
folk
hurrying
along
in

the
gloom
of
night,
as
if
on
the
wings
of
the
wind.

His
haunts
are
not
confined
to
the
valley,
but
extend
at
times
to
the
adjacent
roads,
and
especially
to
the
vicinity
of
a
church
at
no
great
distance.

Indeed,
certain
of
the
most
authentic

historians
of
those
parts,
who
have
been
careful
in
collecting
and
collating
the
floating
facts
concerning
this
spectre,
allege
that
the
body
of
the
trooper
having
been
buried
in
the
churchyard,
the
ghost
rides
forth
to
the
scene
of
battle
in
nightly
quest
of
his
head,
and
that

the
rushing
speed
with
which
he
sometimes
passes
along
the
Hollow,
like
a
midnight
blast,
is
owing
to
his
being
belated,
and
in
a
hurry
to
get
back
to
the
churchyard
before
daybreak.

Such
is
the
general
purport
of
this
legendary
superstition,
which
has
furnished
materials
for

many
a
wild
story
in
that
region
of
shadows;
and
the
spectre
is
known
at
all
the
country
firesides,
by
the
name
of
the
Headless
Horseman
of
Sleepy
Hollow.

It
is
remarkable
that
the
visionary
propensity
I
have
mentioned
is
not
confined
to
the
native
inhabitants
of

the
valley,
but
is
unconsciously
imbibed
by
every
one
who
resides
there
for
a
time.

However
wide
awake
they
may
have
been
before
they
entered
that
sleepy
region,
they
are
sure,
in
a
little
time,
to
inhale
the
witching
influence
of
the
air,
and
begin
to
grow

imaginative,
to
dream
dreams,
and
see
apparitions.

I
mention
this
peaceful
spot
with
all
possible
laud,
for
it
is
in
such
little
retired
Dutch
valleys,
found
here
and
there
embosomed
in
the
great
State
of
New
York,
that
population,
manners,
and
customs
remain
fixed,
while
the
great

torrent
of
migration
and
improvement,
which
is
making
such
incessant
changes
in
other
parts
of
this
restless
country,
sweeps
by
them
unobserved.

They
are
like
those
little
nooks
of
still
water,
which
border
a
rapid
stream,
where
we
may
see
the
straw
and
bubble
riding
quietly
at

anchor,
or
slowly
revolving
in
their
mimic
harbor,
undisturbed
by
the
rush
of
the
passing
current.
Though
many
years
have
elapsed
since
I
trod
the
drowsy
shades
of
Sleepy
Hollow,
yet
I
question
whether
I
should
not
still
find
the
same
trees
and
the
same
families
vegetating
in

its
sheltered
bosom.

In
this
by-place
of
nature
there
abode,
in
a
remote
period
of
American
history,
that
is
to
say,
some
thirty
years
since,
a
worthy
wight
of
the
name
of
Ichabod
Crane,
who
sojourned,
or,
as
he
expressed
it,
"tarried,"
in
Sleepy
Hollow,
for
the

purpose
of
instructing
the
children
of
the
vicinity.

He
was
a
native
of
Connecticut,
a
State
which
supplies
the
Union
with
pioneers
for
the
mind
as
well
as
for
the
forest,
and
sends
forth
yearly
its
legions
of
frontier
woodmen
and
country
schoolmasters.

The
cognomen
of

Crane
was
not
inapplicable
to
his
person.

He
was
tall,
but
exceedingly
lank,
with
narrow
shoulders,
long
arms
and
legs,
hands
that
dangled
a
mile
out
of
his
sleeves,
feet
that
might
have
served
for
shovels,
and
his
whole
frame
most
loosely
hung
together.

His
head
was
small,
and
flat
at
top,
with
huge
ears,
large
green
glassy
eyes,
and
a
long
snipe
nose,
so
that
it
looked
like
a
weather-cock
perched
upon
his
spindle
neck
to
tell
which
way
the
wind
blew.

To
see
him
striding
along
the
profile
of
a
hill
on
a
windy
day,
with
his
clothes
bagging
and
fluttering
about
him,
one
might
have
mistaken
him
for
the
genius
of
famine
descending
upon
the
earth,
or
some
scarecrow
eloped
from
a
cornfield.

His
schoolhouse
was
a
low
building
of
one
large
room,
rudely
constructed
of
logs;
the
windows
partly
glazed,
and
partly
patched
with
leaves
of
old
copybooks.

It
was
most
ingeniously
secured
at
vacant
hours,
by
a
withe
twisted
in
the
handle
of
the
door,
and
stakes
set
against
the
window
shutters;
so
that
though
a
thief
might
get
in
with
perfect

ease,
he
would
find
some
embarrassment
in
getting
out,--an
idea
most
probably
borrowed
by
the
architect,
Yost
Van
Houten,
from
the
mystery
of
an
eelpot.
The
schoolhouse
stood
in
a
rather
lonely
but
pleasant
situation,
just
at
the
foot
of
a
woody
hill,
with
a
brook
running
close

by,
and
a
formidable
birch-tree
growing
at
one
end
of
it.

From
hence
the
low
murmur
of
his
pupils'
voices,
conning
over
their
lessons,
might
be
heard
in
a
drowsy
summer's
day,
like
the
hum
of
a
beehive;
interrupted
now
and
then
by
the
authoritative
voice
of

the
master,
in
the
tone
of
menace
or
command,
or,
peradventure,
by
the
appalling
sound
of
the
birch,
as
he
urged
some
tardy
loiterer
along
the
flowery
path
of
knowledge.

Truth
to
say,
he
was
a
conscientious
man,
and
ever
bore
in
mind
the
golden
maxim,
"Spare

the
rod
and
spoil
the
child."
Ichabod
Crane's
scholars
certainly
were
not
spoiled.

I
would
not
have
it
imagined,
however,
that
he
was
one
of
those
cruel
potentates
of
the
school
who
joy
in
the
smart
of
their
subjects;
on
the
contrary,
he
administered
justice
with
discrimination

rather
than
severity;
taking
the
burden
off
the
backs
of
the
weak,
and
laying
it
on
those
of
the
strong.

Your
mere
puny
stripling,
that
winced
at
the
least
flourish
of
the
rod,
was
passed
by
with
indulgence;
but
the
claims
of
justice
were
satisfied
by
inflicting

a
double
portion
on
some
little
tough
wrong-headed,
broad-skirted
Dutch
urchin,
who
sulked
and
swelled
and
grew
dogged
and
sullen
beneath
the
birch.

All
this
he
called
"doing
his
duty
by
their
parents;"
and
he
never
inflicted
a
chastisement
without
following
it
by
the
assurance,
so
consolatory

to
the
smarting
urchin,
that
"he
would
remember
it
and
thank
him
for
it
the
longest
day
he
had
to
live."

When
school
hours
were
over,
he
was
even
the
companion
and
playmate
of
the
larger
boys;
and
on
holiday
afternoons
would
convoy
some
of
the
smaller

ones
home,
who
happened
to
have
pretty
sisters,
or
good
housewives
for
mothers,
noted
for
the
comforts
of
the
cupboard.

Indeed,
it
behooved
him
to
keep
on
good
terms
with
his
pupils.

The
revenue
arising
from
his
school
was
small,
and
would
have
been
scarcely
sufficient

to
furnish
him
with
daily
bread,
for
he
was
a
huge
feeder,
and,
though
lank,
had
the
dilating
powers
of

an
anaconda;
but
to
help
out
his
maintenance,
he
was,
according
to
country
custom
in
those
parts,
boarded
and
lodged

at
the
houses
of
the
farmers
whose
children
he
instructed.
With
these
he
lived
successively
a
week
at
a
time,

thus
going
the
rounds
of
the
neighborhood,
with
all
his
worldly
effects
tied
up
in
a
cotton
handkerchief.

Now, more than one word per line is presented. Continue to read sweeping your pen or finger down the page as fast as you can take in the story.

That all this
might not be
too onerous
on the purses
of his rustic
patrons, who
are apt to
consider the
costs of
schooling a
grievous
burden, and
schoolmasters
as mere
drones, he had
various ways
of rendering
himself both
useful and
agreeable. He
assisted the

farmers
occasionally in
the lighter
labors of their
farms, helped
to make hay,
mended the
fences, took
the horses to
water, drove
the cows from
pasture, and
cut wood for
the winter fire.
He laid aside,
too, all the
dominant
dignity and
absolute sway
with which he
lorded it in his
little empire,
the school,

and became
wonderfully
gentle and
ingratiating.
He found
favor in the eyes
of the mothers
by petting the
children,
particularly the
youngest; and,
he would sit
with a child on
one knee, and
rock a cradle
with his foot for
whole hours
together.

In addition to
his other

vocations, he
was the
singing-
master of the
neighborhood,
and picked up
many bright
shillings by
instructing the
young folks in
psalmody.
It was a matter
of no little
vanity to him
on Sundays, to
take his
station in
front of the
church gallery,
with a band of
chosen
singers; where,
in his own

mind, he completely carried away the palm from the parson. Certain it is, his voice resounded far above all the rest of the congregation; and there are peculiar quavers still to be heard in that church, and which may even be heard half a mile off, quite to the opposite side of the millpond, on a still Sunday morning, which are said to be legitimately descended from the nose of Ichabod Crane. Thus, by divers little makeshifts, in that ingenious way which is commonly denominated "by hook and by crook," the worthy pedagogue got on tolerably enough, and was thought, by all who

understood nothing of the labor of headwork, to have a wonderfully easy life of it.

The Schoolmaster is generally a man of some importance in the female circle of a rural neighborhood; being considered a kind of idle, gentlemanlike personage, of vastly superior taste and accomplishments to the rough country swains, and, indeed, inferior in learning only to the parson. His appearance, therefore, is apt to occasion some little stir at the tea-table of a farmhouse, and the addition of a Supernumerary dish of cakes or sweetmeats, or,

peradventure, the parade of a silver teapot. Our man of letters, therefore, was peculiarly happy in the smiles of all the country damsels. How he would figure among them in the churchyard, between services on Sundays; gathering grapes for them from the wild vines that overran the surrounding trees; reciting for their amusement all the epitaphs on the tombstones; or sauntering, with a whole bevy of them, along the banks of the adjacent millpond; while the more bashful country bumpkins hung sheepishly back, envying his superior elegance and address.

From his half-itinerant life, also, he was a kind of traveling gazette, carrying the whole budget of local gossip from house to house, so that his appearance was always greeted with satisfaction. He was, moreover, esteemed by the women as a man of great erudition, for he had read several books quite through, and was a perfect master of Cotton Mather's "History of New England Witchcraft," in which, by the way, he most firmly and potently believed.

He was, in fact, an odd mixture of small shrewdness and simple credulity.

His appetite for the marvelous, and his powers of digesting it, were equally extraordinary; and both had been increased by his residence in this spell-bound region. No tale was too gross or monstrous for his capacious swallow. It was often his delight, after his school was dismissed in the afternoon, to stretch himself on the rich bed of clover bordering the little brook that whimpered by his schoolhouse, and there con over old Mather's direful tales, until the gathering dusk of evening made the printed page a mere mist before his eyes.

Then, as he wended his way by swamp and stream and awful woodland, to the farmhouse where he happened to be quartered, every sound of nature, at that witching hour, fluttered his excited imagination, --the moan of the whip-poor-will from the hillside, the boding cry of the tree toad, that harbinger of storm, the dreary hooting of the screech owl, or the sudden rustling in the thicket of birds frightened from their roost. The fireflies, too, which sparkled most vividly in the darkest places, now and then startled him, as one of uncommon brightness would stream across his path; and if,

by chance, a huge blockhead of a beetle came winging his blundering flight against him, the poor varlet was ready to give up the ghost, with the idea that he was struck with a witch's token. His only resource on such occasions, either to drown thought or drive away evil spirits, was to sing psalm tunes and the good people of Sleepy Hollow, as they sat by their doors of an evening, were often filled with awe at hearing his nasal melody, "in linked sweetness long drawn out," floating from the distant hill, or along the dusky road.

Another of his sources of

fearful pleasure was to pass long winter evenings with the old Dutch wives, as they sat spinning by the fire, with a row of apples roasting and spluttering along the hearth, and listen to their marvelous tales of ghosts and goblins, and haunted fields, and haunted brooks, and haunted bridges, and haunted houses, and particularly of the headless horseman, or Galloping Hessian of the Hollow, as they sometimes called him. He would delight them equally by his anecdotes of witchcraft, and of the direful omens and portentous sights and sounds in the air, which prevailed in the earlier times of Connecticut; and would frighten them woefully with speculations upon comets and shooting stars; and with the alarming fact that the world did absolutely turn round, and that they were half the time topsy-turvy!

But if there was a pleasure in all this, while snugly cuddling in the chimney corner of a chamber that was all of a ruddy glow from the crackling wood fire, and where, of course, no spectre dared to show its face, it was dearly purchased by the terrors of his subsequent walk homewards. What fearful shapes and shadows beset his path, amidst the dim and ghastly glare of a snowy night! With what wistful look did he eye every trembling ray of light streaming across the waste fields from some distant window! How often was he appalled by some shrub covered with snow, which, like a sheeted spectre, beset his very path! How often did he shrink with curdling awe at the sound of his own steps on the frosty crust beneath his feet; and dread to look over his shoulder, lest he should behold some uncouth being tramping close behind him! And how often was he thrown into complete dismay by some rushing blast, howling among the trees, in the idea that it was the Galloping Hessian on one of his nightly scourings!

All these, however, were mere terrors of the night, phantoms of the mind that walk in darkness; and though he had seen many specters in his time, and been more than once beset by Satan in divers shapes, in his lonely perambulations, yet daylight put an end to all these evils; and he would have passed a pleasant life of it, in despite of the Devil and all his works, if his path had not been crossed by a being that causes more perplexity to mortal man than ghosts, goblins, and the whole race of witches put together, and that was--a woman.

Among the musical disciples who assembled, one evening in each week, to receive his instructions in psalmody, was Katrina Van Tassel, the daughter and only child of a substantial Dutch farmer.

She was a blooming lass of fresh eighteen; plump as a partridge; ripe and melting and rosy-cheeked as one of her father's peaches, and universally famed, not merely for her beauty, but her vast expectations. She was withal a little of a coquette, as might be perceived even in her dress, which was a mixture of ancient and modern fashions, as most suited to set off her charms. She wore the ornaments of pure yellow gold, which her great-great-grandmother had brought over from Saardam; the tempting stomacher of the olden time, and withal a provokingly short petticoat, to display the prettiest foot and ankle in the country round.

Ichabod Crane had a soft and foolish heart towards the se ; and it is not to be wondered at that so tempting a morsel soon found favor in his eyes, more especially after he had visited her in her paternal mansion.

Old Baltus Van Tassel was a perfect picture of a thriving, contented, liberal-hearted farmer. He seldom, it is true, sent either his eyes or his thoughts beyond the boundaries of his own farm; but within those everything was snug, happy and well-conditioned. He was satisfied with his wealth, but not proud of it; and piqued himself upon the hearty abundance, rather than the style in which he lived.

His stronghold was situated on the banks of the Hudson, in one of those green, sheltered, fertile nooks in which the Dutch farmers are so fond of nestling. A great elm tree spread its broad branches over it, at the foot of which bubbled up a spring of the softest and sweetest water, in a little well formed of a barrel; and then stole sparkling away through the grass, to a neighboring brook, that babbled along among alders and dwarf willows.

Hard by the farmhouse was a vast barn, that might have served for a church; every window and crevice of which seemed bursting forth with the treasures of the farm; the flail was busily resounding within it from morning to night; swallows and martins skimmed twittering about the eaves; and rows of pigeons, some with one eye turned up, as if watching the weather, some with their heads under their wings or buried in their bosoms, and others swelling, and cooing, and bowing about their dames, were enjoying the sunshine on the roof.

Sleek unwieldy porkers were grunting in the repose and abundance of their pens, from whence sallied forth, now and then, troops of sucking pigs, as if to snuff the air. A stately squadron of snowy geese were riding in an adjoining pond, convoying whole fleets of ducks; regiments of turkeys were gobbling through the farmyard, and Guinea fowls fretting about it, like ill-tempered housewives, with their peevish, discontented cry. Before the barn door strutted the gallant cock, that pattern of a

husband, a warrior and a fine gentleman, clapping his burnished wings and crowing in the pride and gladness of his heart,--sometimes tearing up the earth with his feet, and then generously calling his ever-hungry family of wives and children to enjoy the rich morsel which he had discovered.

The pedagogue's mouth watered as he looked upon this sumptuous promise of luxurious winter fare.

In his devouring mind's eye, he pictured to himself every roasting-pig running about with a pudding in his belly, and an apple in his mouth; the pigeons were snugly put to bed in a comfortable pie, and tucked in with a coverlet of crust; the geese were swimming in their own gravy; and the ducks

pairing cozily in dishes, like snug married couples, with a decent competency of onion sauce. In the porkers he saw carved out the future sleek side of bacon, and juicy relishing ham; not a turkey but he beheld daintily trussed up, with its gizzard under its wing, and, peradventure, a necklace of savory sausages; and even bright chanticleer himself lay sprawling on his back, in a side dish, with uplifted claws, as if craving that quarter which his chivalrous spirit disdained to ask while living.

As the enraptured Ichabod fancied all this, and as he rolled his great green eyes over the fat meadow lands, the rich fields of wheat, of rye, of buckwheat, and Indian corn, and the orchards burdened with ruddy fruit, which surrounded the warm tenement of Van Tassel, his heart yearned after the damsel who was to inherit these domains, and his imagination expanded with the idea, how they might be readily turned into cash, and the money invested in immense tracts of wild land, and shingle palaces in the wilderness. Nay, his busy fancy already realized his hopes, and presented to him the blooming Katrina, with a whole family of children, mounted on the top of a wagon loaded with household trumpery, with pots and kettles dangling beneath; and he beheld himself bestriding a pacing mare, with a colt at her heels, setting out for Kentucky, Tennessee,--or the Lord knows where!

When he entered the house, the conquest of his heart was complete. It was one of those spacious farmhouses, with high- ridged but lowly sloping roofs, built in the style handed down from the first Dutch settlers; the low projecting eaves forming a piazza along the front, capable of being closed up in bad weather. Under this were hung flails, harness, various utensils of husbandry, and nets for fishing in the neighboring river. Benches were built along the sides for summer use; and a great spinning-wheel at one end, and a churn at the other, showed the various uses to which this important porch might be devoted. From this piazza the wondering Ichabod entered the hall, which formed the centre of the mansion, and the place of usual residence.

Here rows of resplendent pewter, ranged on a long dresser, dazzled his eyes. In one corner stood a huge bag of wool, ready to be spun; in another, a quantity of linsey-woolsey just from the loom; ears of Indian corn, and strings of dried apples and peaches, hung in gay festoons along the walls, mingled with the gaud of red peppers; and a door left ajar gave him a peep into the best parlor, where the claw-footed chairs and dark mahogany tables shone like mirrors; andirons, with their accompanying shovel and tongs, glistened from their covert of asparagus tops; mock- oranges and conch-shells decorated the mantelpiece; strings of various-colored birds eggs were suspended above it; a great ostrich egg was hung from the centre of the room, and a corner cupboard, knowingly left open, displayed immense treasures of old silver and well-mended china.

From the moment Ichabod laid his eyes upon these regions of delight, the peace of his mind was at an end, and his only study was how to gain the affections of the peerless daughter of Van Tassel.

In this enterprise, however, he had more real difficulties than generally fell to the lot of a knight-errant of yore, who seldom had anything but giants, enchanters, fiery dragons, and such like easily conquered adversaries, to contend with and had to make his way merely through gates of iron and brass, and walls of adamant to the castle keep, where the lady of his heart was confined; all which he achieved as easily as a man would carve his way to the centre of a Christmas pie; and then the lady gave him her hand as a matter of course.

Ichabod, on the contrary, had to win his way to the heart of a country coquette, beset with a labyrinth of whims and caprices, which were forever presenting new difficulties and impediments; and he had to encounter a host of fearful adversaries of real flesh and blood, the numerous rustic admirers, who beset every portal to her heart, keeping a watchful and angry eye upon each other, but ready to fly out in the common cause against any new competitor.

Among these, the most formidable was a burly, roaring, roystering blade, of the name of Abraham, or, according to the Dutch abbreviation, Brom Van Brunt, the hero of the country round, which rang with his feats of strength and hardihood.

He was broad-shouldered and double-jointed, with short curly black hair, and a bluff but not unpleasant countenance, having a mingled air of fun and arrogance.

From his Herculean frame and great powers of limb he had received the nickname of BROM BONES, by which he was universally known.

He was famed for great knowledge and skill in horsemanship, being as dexterous on horseback as a Tartar.

He was foremost at all races and cock fights; and, with the ascendancy which bodily strength always acquires in rustic life, was the umpire in all disputes, setting his hat on one side, and giving his decisions with an air and tone that admitted of no gainsay or appeal.

He was always ready for either a fight or a frolic; but had more mischief than ill-will in his composition; and with all his overbearing roughness, there was a strong dash of waggish good humor at bottom. He had three or four boon companions, who regarded him as their model, and at the head of whom he scoured the country, attending every scene of feud or merriment for miles round. In cold weather he was distinguished by a fur cap, surmounted with a flaunting fox 's tail; and when the folks at a country gathering descried this well-known crest at a distance, whisking about among a squad of hard riders, they always stood by for a squall. Sometimes his crew would be heard dashing along past the farmhouses at midnight, with whoop and halloo, like a troop of Don Cossacks; and the old dames, startled out of their sleep, would listen for a moment till the hurry-scurry had clattered by, and then exclaim, "Ay, there goes Brom Bones and his gang!" The neighbors looked upon him with a mixture of awe, admiration, and good-will; and, when any madcap prank or rustic brawl occurred in the vicinity, always shook their heads, and warranted Brom Bones was at the bottom of it.

This rantipole hero had for some time singled out the blooming Katrina for the object of his uncouth gallantries, and though his amorous toyings were something like the gentle caresses and endearments of a bear, yet it was whispered that she did not altogether discourage his hopes. Certain it is, his advances were signals for rival candidates to retire, who felt no inclination to cross a lion in his amours; insomuch, that when his horse was seen tied to Van Tassel's paling, on a Sunday night, a sure sign that his master was courting, or, as it is termed, "sparking," within, all other suitors passed by in despair, and carried the war into other quarters.

Such was the formidable rival with whom Ichabod Crane had to contend, and, considering all things, a stouter man than he would have shrunk from the competition, and a wiser man

would have despaired.
He had, however, a happy mixture of pliability and perseverance in his nature; he was in form and spirit like a supple-jack--yielding, but tough; though he bent, he never broke; and though he bowed beneath the slightest pressure, yet, the moment it was away--jerk!--he was as erect, and carried his head as high as ever.

To have taken the field openly against his rival would have been madness; for he was not a man to be thwarted in his amours, any more than that stormy lover, Achilles. Ichabod, therefore, made his advances in a quiet and gently insinuating manner. Under cover of his character of singing-master, he made frequent visits at the farmhouse; not that he had anything to

apprehend from the meddlesome interference of parents, which is so often a stumbling-block in the path of lovers. Balt Van Tassel was an easy indulgent soul; he loved his daughter better even than his pipe, and, like a reasonable man and an excellent father, let her have her way in everything. His notable little wife, too, had enough to do to attend to her housekeeping and manage her poultry; for, as she sagely observed, ducks and geese are foolish things, and must be looked after, but girls can take care of themselves. Thus, while the busy dame bustled about the house, or plied her spinning-wheel at one end of the piazza, honest Balt would sit smoking his evening pipe at the other, watching the achievements of a little

wooden warrior, who, armed with a sword in each hand, was most valiantly fighting the wind on the pinnacle of the barn.
In the mean time, Ichabod would carry on his suit with the daughter by the side of the spring under the great elm, or sauntering along in the twilight, that hour so favorable to the lover's eloquence.

I profess not to know how women's hearts are wooed and won. To me they have always been matters of riddle and admiration. Some seem to have but one vulnerable point, or door of access; while others have a thousand avenues, and may be captured in a thousand different ways. It is a great triumph of skill to gain the former, but a still greater proof of generalship to maintain possession of the latter, for man must battle for his fortress at every door and window. He who wins a thousand common hearts is therefore entitled to some renown; but he who keeps undisputed sway over the heart of a coquette is indeed a hero. Certain it is, this was not the case with the redoubtable Brom Bones; and from the moment Ichabod Crane made his advances, the interests of the former evidently declined: his horse was no longer seen tied to the palings on Sunday nights, and a deadly feud gradually arose between him and the preceptor of Sleepy Hollow.

Brom, who had a degree of rough chivalry in his nature, would fain have carried matters to open warfare and have settled their pretensions to the lady, according to the mode of those most concise and simple reasoners, the knights-errant of yore,-- by single combat; but Ichabod was too conscious of the superior might of his adversary to enter the lists against him; he had overheard a boast of Bones, that he would "double the schoolmaster up, and lay him on a shelf of his own schoolhouse;" and he was too wary to give him an opportunity.

There was something extremely provoking in this obstinately pacific system; it left Brom no alternative but to draw upon the funds of rustic waggery in his disposition, and to play off boorish practical jokes upon his rival. Ichabod became the object of whimsical persecution to Bones and his gang of rough riders. They harried his hitherto peaceful domains; smoked out his singing school by stopping up the chimney; broke into the schoolhouse at night, in spite of its formidable fastenings of withe and window stakes, and turned everything topsy-turvy, so that the poor schoolmaster began to think all the witches in the country held their meetings there. But what was still more annoying, Brom took all opportunities of turning him into ridicule in presence of his mistress, and had a scoundrel dog whom he taught to whine in the most ludicrous manner, and introduced as a rival of Ichabod's, to instruct her in psalmody.

In this way matters went on for some time, without producing any material effect on the relative situations of the contending powers. On a fine autumnal afternoon, Ichabod, in pensive mood, sat enthroned on the lofty stool from whence he usually watched all the concerns of his little literary realm.

In his hand he swayed a ferule, that sceptre of despotic power; the birch of justice reposed on three nails behind the throne, a constant terror to evil doers, while on the desk before him might be seen sundry contraband articles and prohibited weapons, detected upon the persons of idle urchins, such as half-munched apples, popguns, whirligigs, fly-cages, and whole legions of rampant little paper gamecocks. Apparently there had been some appalling act of justice recently inflicted, for his scholars were all busily intent upon their books, or slyly whispering behind them with one eye kept upon the master; and a kind of buzzing stillness reigned throughout the schoolroom.

It was suddenly interrupted by the appearance of a negro in tow-cloth jacket and trousers, a round-crowned fragment of a hat, like the cap of Mercury, and mounted on the back of a ragged, wild, half-broken colt, which he managed with a rope by way of halter.

He came clattering up to the school door with an invitation to Ichabod to attend a merry-making or "quilting frolic," to be held that evening at Mynheer Van Tassel's; and having delivered his message with that air of importance, and effort at fine language, which a negro is apt to display on petty embassies of the kind, he dashed over the brook, and

was seen scampering away up the hollow, full of the importance and hurry of his mission.

All was now bustle and hubbub in the late quiet schoolroom. The scholars were hurried through their lessons without stopping at trifles; those who were nimble skipped over half with impunity, and those who were tardy had a smart application now and then in the rear, to quicken their speed or help them over a tall word. Books were flung aside without being put away on the shelves, inkstands were overturned, benches thrown down, and the whole school was turned loose an hour before the usual time, bursting forth like a legion of young imps, yelping and racketing about the green in joy at their early emancipation.

The gallant Ichabod now spent at least an extra half hour at his toilet, brushing and furbishing up his best, and indeed only suit of rusty black, and arranging his locks by a bit of broken looking-glass that hung up in the schoolhouse. That he might make his appearance before his mistress in the true style of a cavalier, he borrowed a horse from the farmer with whom he was staying, a choleric old Dutchman of the name of Hans Van Ripper, and, thus gallantly mounted, issued forth like a knight-errant in quest of adventures.

But it is meet I should, in the true spirit of romantic story, give some account of the looks and equipments of my hero and his steed.

The animal he bestrode was a broken-down plow-horse, that had outlived almost everything but its viciousness.

He was gaunt and shagged, with a ewe neck, and a head like a hammer; his rusty mane and tail were tangled and knotted with burs; one eye had lost its pupil, and was glaring and spectral, but the other had the gleam of a genuine devil in it. Still he must have had fire and mettle in his day, if we may judge from the name he bore of Gunpowder. He had, in fact, been a favorite steed of his master's, the choleric Van Ripper, who was a furious rider, and had infused, very probably, some of his own spirit into the animal; for, old and broken-down as he looked, there was more of the lurking devil in him than in any young filly in the country.

Ichabod was a suitable figure for such a steed. He rode with short stirrups, which brought his knees nearly up to the pommel of the saddle; his sharp elbows stuck out like grasshoppers'; he carried his whip perpendicularly in his hand, like a

sceptre, and as his horse jogged on, the motion of his arms was not unlike the flapping of a pair of wings. A small wool hat rested on the top of his nose, for so his scanty strip of forehead might be called, and the skirts of his black coat fluttered out almost to the horses tail. Such was the appearance of Ichabod and his steed as they shambled out of the gate of Hans Van Ripper, and it was altogether such an apparition as is seldom to be met with in broad daylight.

It was, as I have said, a fine autumnal day; the sky was clear and serene, and nature wore that rich and golden livery which we always associate with the idea of abundance. The forests had put on their sober brown and yellow, while some trees of the tenderer kind had been nipped by the frosts into brilliant dyes of

orange, purple, and scarlet. Streaming files of wild ducks began to make their appearance high in the air; the bark of the squirrel might be heard from the groves of beech and hickory- nuts, and the pensive whistle of the quail at intervals from the neighboring stubble field.

The small birds were taking their farewell banquets. In the fullness of their revelry, they fluttered, chirping and frolicking from bush to bush, and tree to tree, capricious from the very profusion and variety around them. There was the honest cock robin, the favorite game of stripling sportsmen, with its loud querulous note; and the twittering blackbirds flying in sable clouds; and the golden-winged woodpecker with his crimson crest, his broad black gorget, and splendid plumage; and the cedar bird, with its red-tipped wings and yellow-tipped tail and its little monteiro cap of feathers; and the blue jay, that noisy co comb, in his gay light blue coat and white underclothes, screaming and chattering, nodding and bobbing and bowing, and pretending to be on good terms with every songster of the grove.

As Ichabod jogged slowly on his way, his eye, ever open to every symptom of culinary abundance, ranged with delight over the treasures of jolly autumn. On all sides he beheld vast store of apples; some hanging in oppressive opulence on the trees; some gathered into baskets and barrels for the market; others heaped up in rich piles for the cider-press. Farther on he beheld great fields of Indian corn, with its golden ears' peeping from their leafy coverts, and holding out the promise of cakes

and hasty- pudding; and the yellow pumpkins lying beneath them, turning up their fair round bellies to the sun, and giving ample prospects of the most luxurious of pies; and anon he passed the fragrant buckwheat fields breathing the odor of the beehive, and as he beheld them, soft anticipations stole over his mind of dainty slapjacks, well buttered, and garnished with honey or treacle, by the delicate little dimpled hand of Katrina Van Tassel.

Thus feeding his mind with many sweet thoughts and "sugared suppositions," he journeyed along the sides of a range of hills which look out upon some of the goodliest scenes of the mighty Hudson. The sun gradually wheeled his broad disk down in the west. The wide bosom of the Tappan Zee lay motionless and glassy, excepting that here and there a gentle undulation

waved and prolonged the blue shadow of the distant mountain. A few amber clouds floated in the sky, without a breath of air to move them. The horizon was of a fine golden tint, changing gradually into a pure apple green, and from that into the deep blue of the mid- heaven. A slanting ray lingered on the woody crests of the precipices that overhung some parts of the river, giving greater depth to the dark gray and purple of their rocky sides. A sloop was loitering in the distance, dropping slowly down with the tide, her sail hanging uselessly against the mast; and as the reflection of the sky gleamed along the still water, it seemed as if the vessel was suspended in the air.

It was toward evening that Ichabod arrived at the castle of the Heer Van Tassel, which he found thronged with the pride and flower of the adjacent country.

Old farmers, a spare leathern- faced race, in homespun coats and breeches, blue stockings, huge shoes, and magnificent pewter buckles.

Their brisk, withered little dames, in close- crimped caps, long- waisted short gowns, homespun petticoats, with scissors and pincushions, and gay calico pockets hanging on the outside.

Buxom lasses, almost as antiquated as their mothers, excepting where a straw hat, a fine ribbon, or perhaps a white frock, gave symptoms of city innovation.

The sons, in short square-skirted coats, with rows of stupendous brass buttons, and their hair generally queued in the fashion of the times, especially if they could procure an eel-skin for the purpose, it being esteemed throughout the country as a potent nourisher and

strengthener of the hair.

Brom Bones, however, was the hero of the scene, having come to the gathering on his favorite steed Daredevil, a creature, like himself, full of mettle and mischief, and which no one but himself could manage.

He was, in fact, noted for preferring vicious animals, given to all kinds of tricks which kept the rider in constant risk of his neck, for he held a tractable, well-broken horse as unworthy of a lad of spirit.

Fain would I pause to dwell upon the world of charms that burst upon the enraptured gaze of my hero, as he entered the state parlor of Van Tassel's mansion. Not those of the bevy of buxom lasses, with their luxurious display of red and white; but the ample charms of a genuine Dutch

country tea-table, in the sumptuous time of autumn.

Such heaped up platters of cakes of various and almost indescribable kinds, known only to experienced Dutch housewives! There was the doughty doughnut, the tender oly koek, and the crisp and crumbling cruller; sweet cakes and short cakes, ginger cakes and honey cakes, and the whole family of cakes.

And then there were apple pies, and peach pies, and pumpkin pies; besides slices of ham and smoked beef; and moreover delectable dishes of preserved plums, and peaches, and pears, and quinces; not to mention broiled shad and roasted chickens; together with bowls of milk and cream, all mingled higgledy- piggledy, pretty much as I have enumerated them, with the motherly teapot sending up its clouds of vapor from the midst-- Heaven bless the mark! I want breath and time to discuss this banquet as it deserves, and am too eager to get on with my story. Happily, Ichabod Crane was not in so

great a hurry as his historian, but did ample justice to every dainty.

He was a kind and thankful creature, whose heart dilated in proportion as his skin was filled with good cheer, and whose spirits rose with eating, as some men's do with drink. He could not help, too, rolling his large eyes round him as he ate, and chuckling with the possibility that he might one day be lord of all this scene of almost unimaginable luxury and splendor. Then, he thought, how soon he'd . turn his back upon the old schoolhouse; snap his fingers in the face of Hans Van Ripper, and every other niggardly patron, and kick any itinerant pedagogue out of doors that should dare to call him comrade!

Old Baltus Van Tassel moved about among his guests with a face dilated with content and good

humor, round and jolly as the harvest moon. His hospitable attentions were brief, but expressive, being confined to a shake of the hand, a slap on the shoulder, a loud laugh, and a pressing invitation to "fall to, and help themselves."

And now the sound of the music from the common room, or hall, summoned to the dance. The musician was an old gray-headed negro, who had been the itinerant orchestra of the neighborhood for more than half a century. His instrument was as old and battered as himself. The greater part of the time he scraped on two or three strings, accompanying every movement of the bow with a motion of the head; bowing almost to the ground, and stamping with his foot

whenever a fresh couple were to start.

Ichabod prided himself upon his dancing as much as upon his vocal powers. Not a limb, not a fibre about him was idle; and to have seen his loosely hung frame in full motion, and clattering about the room, you would have thought St. Vitus himself, that blessed patron of the dance, was figuring before you in person. He was the admiration of all the negroes; who, having gathered, of all ages and sizes, from the farm and the neighborhood, stood forming a pyramid of shining black faces at every door and window, gazing with delight at the scene, rolling their white eyeballs, and showing grinning rows of ivory from ear to ear. How could the flogger of urchins be otherwise than animated and joyous? The lady of his heart was his partner in the dance, and smiling graciously in reply to all his amorous oglings; while Brom Bones, sorely smitten with love and jealousy, sat brooding by himself in one corner.

When the dance was at an end, Ichabod was attracted to a knot of the sager folks, who, with Old Van Tassel, sat smoking at one end of the piazza, gossiping over former times, and drawing out long stories about the war.

This neighborhood, at the time of which I am speaking, was one of those highly favored places which abound with chronicle and great men.

The British and American line had run near it during the war; it had, therefore, been the scene of marauding and infested with refugees, cowboys, and all kinds of border chivalry. Just sufficient time had elapsed to enable each storyteller to dress up his tale with a little becoming fiction, and, in the indistinctness of his recollection, to make

himself the hero of every exploit.

There was the story of Doffue Martling, a large blue-bearded Dutchman, who had nearly taken a British frigate with an old iron nine-pounder from a mud breastwork, only that his gun burst at the sixth discharge. And there was an old gentleman who shall be nameless, being too rich a mynheer to be lightly mentioned, who, in the battle of White Plains, being an excellent master of defense, parried a musket-ball with a small sword, insomuch that he absolutely felt it whiz round the blade, and glance off at the hilt; in proof of which he was ready at any time to show the sword, with the hilt a little bent. There were several more that had been equally great in the field, not one of whom but was persuaded that he had a considerable hand in bringing the war to a happy termination.

But all these were nothing to the tales of ghosts and apparitions that succeeded.

The neighborhood is rich in legendary treasures of the kind. Local tales and superstitions thrive best in these sheltered, long-settled retreats; but are trampled under foot by the shifting throng that forms the population of most of our country places.

Besides, there is no encouragement for ghosts in most of our villages, for they have scarcely had time to finish their first nap and turn themselves in their graves, before their surviving friends have traveled away from the neighborhood; so that when they turn out at night to walk their rounds, they have no acquaintance left to call upon.

This is perhaps the reason why we so seldom hear of ghosts except in our long-established Dutch communities.

The immediate cause, however, of the prevalence of supernatural stories in these parts, was doubtless owing to the vicinity of Sleepy Hollow.

There was a contagion in the very air that blew from that haunted region; it breathed forth an atmosphere of dreams and fancies infecting all the land. Several of the Sleepy Hollow people were present at Van Tassel's, and, as usual, were doling out their wild and wonderful legends. Many dismal tales were told about funeral trains, and mourning cries and wailings heard and seen about the great tree where the unfortunate Major André was taken, and which stood in the neighborhood. Some mention was made also of the woman in white, that haunted the dark glen at Raven Rock, and was often heard to shriek on winter nights before a storm, having perished there in the snow.

The chief part of the stories, however, turned upon the favorite spectre of Sleepy Hollow, the Headless Horseman, who had been heard several times of late, patrolling the country; and, it was said, tethered his horse nightly among the graves in the churchyard.

The sequestered situation of this church seems always to have made it a favorite haunt of troubled spirits.

It stands on a knoll, surrounded by locust-trees and lofty elms, from among which its decent, whitewashed walls shine modestly forth, like Christian purity beaming through the shades of retirement. A gentle slope descends from it to a silver sheet of water, bordered by high trees, between which, peeps may be caught at the blue hills of the Hudson. To look upon its grass-grown yard, where the sunbeams seem to sleep so quietly, one would think that there at least the dead might rest in peace.

On one side of the church extends a wide woody dell, along which raves a large brook among broken rocks and trunks of fallen trees. Over a deep black part of the stream, not far from the church, was formerly thrown a wooden bridge; the road that led to it, and the bridge itself, were thickly shaded by overhanging trees, which cast a gloom about it, even in the daytime; but occasioned a fearful darkness at night.

Such was one of the favorite haunts of the Headless Horseman, and the place where he was most frequently encountered. The tale was told of old Brouwer, a most heretical disbeliever in ghosts, how he met the Horseman returning from his foray into Sleepy Hollow, and was obliged to get up behind him; how they galloped over bush and brake, over hill and swamp, until they reached the bridge; when the Horseman suddenly turned into a skeleton, threw old Brouwer into the brook, and sprang away over the tree-tops with a clap of thunder.

This story was immediately matched by a thrice marvelous adventure of Brom Bones, who made light of the Galloping Hessian as an arrant jockey. He affirmed that on returning one night from the neighboring village of Sing Sing, he had been overtaken by this midnight trooper; that he had offered to race with him for a bowl of punch, and should have won it too, for Daredevil beat the goblin horse all hollow, but just as they came to the church bridge, the Hessian bolted, and vanished in a flash of fire.

All these tales, told in that drowsy undertone with which men talk in the dark, the countenances of the listeners only now and then receiving a casual gleam from the glare of a pipe, sank deep in the mind of Ichabod.

He repaid them in kind with large extracts from his invaluable author, Cotton Mather, and added many marvelous events that had taken place in his native State of Connecticut, and fearful sights which he had seen in his nightly walks about Sleepy Hollow.

The revel now gradually broke up.

The old farmers gathered together their families in their wagons, and were heard for some time rattling along the hollow roads, and over the distant hills. Some of the damsels mounted on pillions behind their favorite swains, and their light-hearted laughter, mingling with the clatter of hoofs, echoed along the silent woodlands, sounding fainter and fainter, until they gradually died away,--and the late scene of noise and frolic was all silent and deserted. Ichabod only lingered behind, according to the custom of country lovers, to have a tête-à-tête with the heiress; fully convinced that he was now on the high road to success.

What passed at this interview I will not pretend to say, for in fact I do not know. Something, however, I fear me, must have gone wrong, for he certainly sallied forth, after no very great interval, with an air quite desolate and chapfallen.

Oh, these women! these women! Could that girl have been playing off any of her coquettish tricks? Was her encouragement of the poor pedagogue all a mere sham to secure her conquest of his rival? Heaven only knows, not I! Let it suffice to say, Ichabod stole forth with the air of one who had been sacking a henroost, rather than a fair lady's heart.

Without looking to the right or left to notice the scene of rural wealth, on which he had so often gloated, he went straight to the stable, and with several hearty cuffs and kicks roused his steed most uncourteously from the comfortable quarters in which he was soundly sleeping, dreaming of mountains of corn and oats, and whole valleys of timothy and clover.

It was the very witching time of night that Ichabod, heavy-hearted and crestfallen, pursued his travels homewards, along the sides of the lofty hills which rise above Tarry Town, and which he had traversed so cheerily in the afternoon.

The hour was as dismal as himself.

Far below him the Tappan Zee spread its dusky and indistinct waste of waters, with here and there the tall mast of a sloop, riding quietly at anchor under the land.

In the dead hush of midnight, he could even hear the barking of the watchdog from the opposite shore of the Hudson; but it was so vague and faint as only to give an idea of his distance from this faithful companion of man.

Now and then, too, the long-drawn crowing of a cock, accidentally awakened, would sound far, far off, from some farmhouse away among the hills--but it was like a dreaming sound in his ear.

No signs of life occurred near him, but occasionally the melancholy chirp of a cricket, or perhaps the guttural twang of a bullfrog from a neighboring marsh, as if sleeping uncomfortably and turning suddenly in his bed.

All the stories of ghosts and goblins that he had heard in the afternoon now came crowding upon his recollection. The night grew darker and darker; the stars seemed to sink deeper in the sky, and driving clouds occasionally hid them from his sight. He had never felt so lonely and dismal. He was, moreover, approaching the very place where many of the scenes of the ghost stories had been laid. In the centre of the road stood an enormous tulip-tree,

which towered like a giant above all the other trees of the neighborhood, and formed a kind of landmark. Its limbs were gnarled and fantastic, large enough to form trunks for ordinary trees, twisting down almost to the earth, and rising again into the air.

It was connected with the tragical story of the unfortunate André, who had been taken prisoner hard by; and was universally known by the name of Major André's tree. The common people regarded it with a mixture of respect and superstition, partly out of sympathy for the fate of its ill- starred namesake, and partly from the tales of strange sights, and doleful lamentations, told concerning it.

As Ichabod approached this fearful tree, he began to whistle; he thought his whistle was answered; it was but a blast sweeping sharply through the dry branches.

As he approached a little nearer, he thought he saw

something white, hanging in the midst of the tree: he paused and ceased whistling but, on looking more narrowly, perceived that it was a place where the tree had been scathed by lightning, and the white wood laid bare. Suddenly he heard a groan--his teeth chattered, and his knees smote against the saddle: it was but the rubbing of one huge bough upon another, as they were swayed about by the breeze.

He passed the tree in safety, but new perils lay before him.

About two hundred yards from the tree, a small brook crossed the road, and ran into a marshy and thickly-wooded glen, known by the name of Wiley's Swamp.

A few rough logs, laid side by side, served for a bridge over this stream.

On that side of the road where the brook entered the wood, a group of oaks and chestnuts, matted thick with wild grape-vines, threw a cavernous gloom over it.

To pass this bridge was the severest trial. It was at this identical spot that the unfortunate André was captured, and under the covert of those chestnuts and vines were the sturdy yeomen concealed who surprised him. This has ever since been considered a haunted stream, and fearful are the feelings of the schoolboy who has to pass it alone after dark.

As he approached the stream, his heart began to thump; he summoned up, however, all his resolution, gave his horse half a score of kicks in the ribs, and attempted to dash briskly across the bridge; but instead of starting forward, the perverse old animal made a lateral movement, and ran broadside against the fence.

Ichabod, whose fears increased with the delay, jerked the reins on the other side, and kicked lustily with the contrary foot: it was all in vain; his steed started, it is true, but it was only to plunge to the opposite side of the road into a thicket of brambles and alder bushes.

The schoolmaster now bestowed both whip and heel upon the starveling ribs of old Gunpowder, who dashed forward, snuffling and snorting, but came to a stand just by the bridge, with a suddenness that had nearly sent his rider sprawling over his head.

Just at this moment a plashy tramp by the side of the bridge caught the sensitive ear of Ichabod.

In the dark shadow of the grove, on the margin of the brook, he beheld something huge, misshapen and towering.

It stirred not, but seemed gathered up in the gloom, like some gigantic monster ready to spring upon the traveler.

The hair of the affrighted pedagogue rose upon his head with terror.

What was to be done? To turn and fly was now too late; and besides, what chance was there of escaping ghost or goblin, if such it was, which could ride upon the wings of the wind?

Summoning up, therefore, a show of courage, he demanded in stammering accents, "Who are you?" He received no reply.

He repeated his demand in a still more agitated voice.

Still there was no answer.

Once more he cudgeled the sides of the inflexible Gunpowder, and, shutting his eyes, broke forth with involuntary fervor into a psalm tune.

Just then the shadowy object of alarm put itself in motion, and with a scramble and a bound stood at once in the middle of the road.

Though the night was dark and dismal, yet the form of the unknown might now in some degree be ascertained.

He appeared to be a horseman of large dimensions, and mounted on a black horse of powerful frame.

He made no offer of molestation or sociability, but kept aloof on one side of the road, jogging along on the blind side of old Gunpowder, who had now got over his fright and waywardness.

Ichabod, who had no relish for this strange midnight companion, and bethought himself of the adventure of Brom Bones with the Galloping Hessian, now quickened his steed in hopes of leaving him behind. The stranger, however, quickened his horse to an equal pace. Ichabod pulled up, and fell into a walk, thinking to lag behind,--the other did the same. His heart began to sink within him; he endeavored to resume his psalm tune, but his parched tongue clove to the roof of his mouth, and he could not utter a stave. There was something in the moody and dogged silence of this companion that was mysterious and appalling. It was soon fearfully accounted for. On mounting a rising ground, which brought the figure of his fellow-traveler in relief against the sky, gigantic in height, and muffled in a cloak, Ichabod was horror-struck on perceiving that he was headless!-- but his horror was still more increased on observing that the head, which should have rested on his shoulders, was carried before him on the pommel of his saddle! His terror rose to desperation; he rained a shower of kicks and blows upon Gunpowder, hoping by a sudden movement to give his companion the slip; but the spectre started full jump with him. Away, then, they dashed through thick and thin; stones flying and sparks flashing at every bound. Ichabod's flimsy garments fluttered in the air, as he stretched his long lank body away over his horse's head, in the eagerness of his flight.

They had now reached the road which turns off to Sleepy Hollow; but Gunpowder, who seemed possessed with a demon, instead of keeping up it, made an opposite turn, and plunged headlong downhill to the left. This road leads through a sandy hollow shaded by trees for about a quarter of a mile, where it crosses the bridge famous in goblin story; and just beyond swells the green knoll on which stands the whitewashed church.

As yet the panic of the steed had given his unskillful rider an apparent advantage in the chase, but just as he had got half way through the hollow, the girths of the saddle gave way, and he felt it slipping from under him. He seized it by the pommel, and endeavored to hold it firm, but in vain; and had just time to save himself by clasping old Gunpowder round the neck, when the saddle fell to the earth, and he heard it trampled under foot by his pursuer. For a moment the terror of Hans Van Ripper's wrath passed across his mind,--for it was his Sunday saddle; but this was no time for petty fears; the goblin was hard on his haunches; and (unskillful rider that he was!) he had much ado to maintain his seat; sometimes slipping on one side, sometimes on another, and sometimes jolted on the high ridge of his horse's backbone, with

a violence that he verily feared would cleave him asunder.

An opening in the trees now cheered him with the hopes that the church bridge was at hand. The wavering reflection of a silver star in the bosom of the brook told him that he was not mistaken. He saw the walls of the church dimly glaring under the trees beyond. He recollected the place where Brom Bones's ghostly competitor had disappeared. "If I can but reach that bridge," thought Ichabod, "I am safe." Just then he heard the black steed panting and blowing close behind him; he even fancied that he felt his hot breath. Another convulsive kick in the ribs, and old Gunpowder sprang upon the bridge; he thundered over the resounding planks; he gained the opposite side; and now Ichabod cast a look behind to see if his pursuer should vanish, according to rule, in a flash of fire and brimstone. Just then he saw the goblin rising in his stirrups, and in the very act of hurling his head at him. Ichabod endeavored to dodge the horrible missile, but too late. It encountered his cranium with a tremendous crash,--he was tumbled headlong into the dust, and Gunpowder, the black steed, and the goblin rider, passed by like a whirlwind.

The next morning the old horse was found without his saddle, and with the bridle under his feet, soberly cropping the grass at his master's gate. Ichabod did not make his appearance at breakfast; dinner-hour came, but no Ichabod. The boys assembled at the schoolhouse, and strolled idly about the banks of the brook; but no schoolmaster. Hans Van Ripper now began to feel some uneasiness about the fate of poor Ichabod, and his saddle. An inquiry was set on foot, and after diligent investigation they came upon his traces. In one part of the road leading to the church was found the saddle trampled in the dirt; the tracks of horses' hoofs deeply dented in the road, and evidently at furious speed, were traced to the bridge, beyond which, on the bank of a broad part of the brook, where the water ran deep and black, was found the hat of the unfortunate Ichabod, and close beside it a shattered pumpkin.

The brook was searched, but the body of the schoolmaster was not to be discovered.

Hans Van Ripper as executor of his estate, examined the bundle which contained all his worldly effects.

They consisted of two shirts and a half; two stocks for the neck; a pair or two of worsted stockings; an old pair of corduroy small- clothes; a rusty razor; a book of psalm tunes full of dog's-ears; and a broken pitch-pipe.

As to the books and furniture of the schoolhouse, they belonged to the community, excepting Cotton Mather's "History of Witchcraft," a "New England Almanac," and a book of dreams and fortune-telling; in which last was a sheet of foolscap much scribbled and blotted in several fruitless attempts to make a copy of verses in honor of the heiress of Van Tassel. These magic books and the poetic scrawl were forthwith consigned to the flames by Hans Van Ripper; who, from that time forward, determined to send his children no more to school, observing that he never knew any good come of this same reading and writing.

Whatever money the schoolmaster possessed, and he had received his quarter's pay but a day or two before, he must have had about his person at the time of his disappearance.

The mysterious event caused much speculation at the church on the following Sunday.

Knots of gazers and gossips were collected in the churchyard, at the bridge, and at the spot where the hat and pumpkin had been found.

The stories of Brouwer, of Bones, and a whole budget of others were called to mind; and when they had diligently considered them all, and compared them with the symptoms of the present case, they shook their heads, and came to the conclusion that Ichabod had been carried off by the Galloping Hessian.

As he was a bachelor, and in nobody's debt, nobody troubled his head any more about him; the school was removed to a different quarter of the hollow, and another pedagogue reigned in his stead.

It is true, an old farmer, who had been down to New York on a visit several years after, and from whom this account of the ghostly adventure was received, brought home the intelligence that Ichabod Crane was still alive; that he had left the neighborhood partly through fear of the goblin and Hans Van Ripper, and partly in mortification at having been suddenly dismissed by the heiress; that he had changed his quarters to a distant part of the country; had kept school and studied law at the same time; had been admitted to the bar; turned politician; electioneered; written for the newspapers; and finally had been made a justice of the Ten Pound Court.

Brom Bones, too, who, shortly after his rival's disappearance conducted the blooming Katrina in triumph to the altar, was observed to look exceedingly knowing whenever the story of Ichabod was related, and always burst into a hearty laugh at the mention of the pumpkin; which led some to suspect that he knew more about the matter than he chose to tell.

The old country wives, however, who are the best judges of these matters, maintain to this day that Ichabod was spirited away by supernatural means; and it is a favorite story often told about the neighborhood round the winter evening fire.
The bridge became more than ever an object of superstitious awe; and that may be the reason why the road has been altered of late years, so as to approach the church by the border of the millpond.

The schoolhouse being deserted soon fell to decay, and was reported to be haunted by the ghost of the unfortunate pedagogue and the plowboy, loitering homeward of a still summer evening, has often fancied his voice at a distance, chanting a melancholy psalm tune among the tranquil solitudes of Sleepy Hollow.

The End.

CHAPTER 8

Using your computer to SPEED-Train

Learn how to make your computer to mimic an expensive tachistoscopic machine. Set up your computer so it can act as your trainer, flashing words and phrases at you in a manner that will help accelerate your reading.

You can adjust your computer to mimic very expensive tachistoscopic machines. These machines and computer programs are designed to accelerate your reading. They present text to you by a method called "Rapid Serial Visualization Process" or RSVP for short. A word or group of words is shown to you on a screen for a fraction of a second. These words are then replaced with the next word or words to be read.

They train you to read quicker in two ways:

1. **Increasing the words per focus**
    They can increase the number of words the eye can take in with each focus. They do this by increasing the number of words that appear with each flash. For instance, initially it is usual to be only able to take in about a word with each flash but with practice two words may be taken in, then three, etc.

2. **Decreasing the time required per focus**
    As you progress each word or group of words is presented / flashed for a shorter time period. This way the eyes get used to taking in information more quickly.

To mimic these machines / software on your computer you need to:
*   Set your screen up properly
*   Adjust the speed of each flash

These instructions are for Microsoft Windows but by a similar mechanism you should be able to configure most operating systems for speed training.

Using your text editor, (e.g. Microsoft Word or WordPad) open up the document you wish to practice on, e.g. a short story.

Setting up your screen:

The aim is to have just **one line of very large text** on your screen.

1. Select the entire document, choose a clear font, e.g. **Tahoma**, and set the **font size to 72**. The text should now appear huge on your screen.
2. Reduce the number of lines to just **one line** of text. You do this by making the screen smaller until it contains just one line of the huge text.

(To make a screen smaller just place the cursor over the top or bottom edge of the application – the cursor changes to a double arrow - and drag the edge making it smaller).

Your screen should look something like this now:

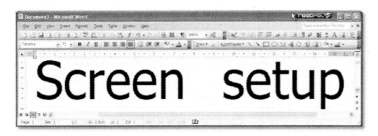

You can increase the words per line by decreasing the font size. You can decrease the words per line by adjusting the page margin.

Now just use the down arrow to move through the document. This will replace the first line of text with the next. Keep the down arrow pressed and each line of text should be replaced with the next. Each line flashes up.

Note this is different from scrolling where the text is continuously moved up the screen. Scrolling is difficult to read as the eye needs a fixed object to focus on. Each line should not roll up the screen but simply be *replaced* by the next. For the proper replacement to happen the window size needs to be one line deep, no more, no less. Adjust it until scrolling does not happen.

Adjusting the speed

The easiest way to adjust your speed is to adjust the repeat rate in keyboard properties. This is how to do that:

Click on the Start button, bottom left of your screen.
Click on Control Panel
Click on Keyboard

Within 'Keyboard' in the Speed Menu there is a slider that controls the repeat rate.

Within 'Keyboard' in the Speed menu there is a slider that controls the repeat rate.

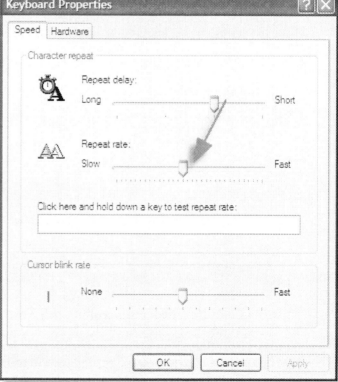

Adjust this slider and see its effects on your reading speed in the editor / document you have prepared for speed reading training. Keep your finger on the down arrow to move through the document. (Initially you will need to adjust the rate quite often so you should keep Keyboard Properties open).

Now you are ready to start speed training using your computer.

SPEED TRAINING WITH YOUR COMPUTER

Exercise 3

As with training on printed material you try to read beyond your present capabilities. You then reread at a higher speed and then again at an even greater speed. This challenges the brain. You adapt and start reading more quickly with the same level of understanding as before, (and often with improved understanding).

Prepare for your training sessions as outlined above. Choose a short story or a document you want to read anyway. Adjust the Font Size and the Repeat Rate so that you are able to read comfortably.

1. Increase the number of words per line. You can do this most easily by decreasing the font size, (to the next level down). Or, if this jump is too big you can reset the page width / margins, (as ever, be sure that each line is being replaced not scrolled). Now read the text by pressing the down arrow key. You should have difficulty reading at this speed but be able to make out some of what is being said. Read to the end of the story.

Return the font to the original size. (Control + z will usually undo these changes).

2. Re-read the story at higher speed. Adjust the Repeat rate up. Normally two notches on the slider is an appropriate increase. You should have difficulty reading at this speed but be able to make out some of what is being said.

3. Now re-read the story at both increased Repeat Rate and increased words-per-line. This will be difficult. But persevere! *Great speed comes to those who train at great speed.*

Exercise 4, Visual Span Exercise

Minute for minute this is probably the most effective of all the speed-reading exercises. It is designed to increase your visual span, the number of words that you can take in with each focusing of your eyes.

Interestingly, these exercises are very similar to those that elite sportsmen and women do to improve their peripheral vision. Peripheral vision is very important in sports like tennis or soccer where you might have to pick out the goal or a teammate with the corner of you eye.

In these exercises you are briefly presented with a row of words or numbers. One of these is repeated, you just have to decide which. Sounds simple... but try doing it at high speed on level 6!

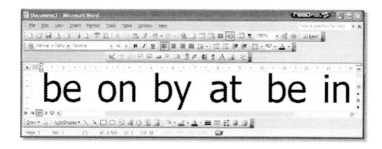

The files for all these exercises are available for free from www.readpal.com
Go to the speed section of the ReadPal website and look for Visual Span Exercises.

Open Visual Span Exercise, Level 1.
Adjust the screen size of your editor, (e.g. Microsoft Word) so that only **one full line of text** appears. Then use the down arrow to move through the document. As before, make sure the lines do not scroll but rather replace one another.

A line of numbers or words will flash up, mentally note which word or number appeared twice, you will then be shown the right answer. Set the Repeat Rate, as above, so that you are just able to keep up. Try to look at the whole line of text in one focus. (I.e. do not take in the line in two goes, if you need to do that you should move down a level). Once you are comfortable doing it at high speed move up to the next level.

Below is a taste of the text in the exercises:

Level 1

Which word is repeated?

be   is   be

be   was repeated

Level 6.

Which number is repeated?

8985   1349   1223   1598   4968   4968

4968   was repeated.

You should practice at least one of the computer based exercises everyday for the duration of the course.

Part III
Skimming

Efficient skimming is a valuable skill.

This section has two parts.

1. An overview of skimming techniques on print material for study and work.

2. Exercises to improve your skimming and overall reading speed.

Chapter 9

Overview and Skimming

In this short chapter we examine skimming, skimming techniques and give you an exercise to improve your skimming ability.

The skills of skimming are of benefit if you want to:

- Get a quick idea of what an article or book is about
- Increase your regular speed by encouraging you to push your limits
- Finish double-quick - you got no time!
- Develop habits that will help you understanding a document thoroughly
- As part of a Study routine, see the chapter on Study Techniques

When catching absolutely every word is not of critical importance you have the luxury of skimming. You go through a document, very quickly, picking out what is important to get the gist of what is being said.

There are general guidelines to assist you:

- Read headings, *italics*, **bolds**, <u>underlined</u> and CAPITALISED words

- Pay more attention to the first and last paragraph

- If there is a summary or overview... don't be foolish... read it well

- Pay more attention to the first and last sentence of a paragraph

- Know that most words are unimportant to the overall meaning and can be glossed over.

Exercise 5

Pick out several documents you would like / need to read. Using your finger or pen as a pacer go through the document at three times your regular speed skipping along, paying most attention to the areas mentioned above. Do not attempt to read full sentences. Pick out snippets and key words to form an opinion of what the author was trying to say. When you have finished the document jot down the key points. Use short-hand / abbreviations, this should only take a couple of minutes. Then reread the document as fast as you can, for good comprehension, checking how good your skimming is. As you practise with this technique you will find your skimming skills improving.

"The art of reading is to skip judiciously".

Philip Gilbert Hamerton

Chapter 10

An exercise in the unimportance of words!

The exercise in this chapter is designed to give you practice and confidence in skimming and pushing your reading speed to new levels.

Unimportant words:

'A' is a word that should be beloved only by dreamers and poets...

Some words are unimportant and unnecessarily slow us down when we are reading. They add nothing to our meaning - they just take up space and our time. 'The' and 'a' are among the most common words, yet some Far Eastern languages do not even have an equivalent. In fact, in English they are superfluous except when you really want to emphasise something and then they are usually italicised, e.g. '*the* man'.

In Spanish they do not usually bother with personal pronouns, (I, you, he, she, etc.), when they do it is for emphasis, as in '*he* did it'. So 'habla' could mean he speaks, she speaks or it speaks. From the context it is usually evident... they don't waste our time explaining which.

You can read laboriously "The cat sat on the mat", however, with a little practice " cat sat   mat" would be just as easy to understand. The mind fills in the blanks. Luckily, it finds this even easier to do at high speeds. The mind gets in a groove and picks what is necessary for understanding.

Usually verbs and nouns are the most important for comprehension.   Adverbs, adjectives, qualifiers, conjunctions and the definite and indefinite articles are of little value. (There are, of course, a few notable exceptions. Words indicating opposite or words that alter the direction of a sentence.   For example NOT can be very important. Try telling someone "I do love you" then "I do NOT love you").

The next exercise is designed to help you:

1. Develop the skill of skimming
2. As a speed exercise; push your skimming limits and then reread them at your top speed
3. Eliminate excessive subvocalisation – it's more difficult to say words that aren't there!

> *"There is creative reading as well as creative writing."*
> **Ralph Waldo Emerson**

In Exercise 6 unimportant words are replaced with an x. Do NOT concentrate on or try to substitute the missing words. Just skip them and certainly don't say them.

As you progress through the story more words are replaced. Use your index finger to keep your pace up. Be sure to read it at a good speed... later on you can always re-read it.

Do not expect to catch the *exact* meaning of every sentence. This is an exercise to show how easy it can be to catch the overall thrust and meaning at speed. With practice you become progressively better at it.

(This practice is also useful for those learning a foreign language. Those skilled at 'filling in the blanks' will have a big advantage when it comes to reading foreign languages where many words may be unknown).

(The patented AutoSkim™ software from ReadPal can automatically remove up to 50% of the words enabling you to skim any document more quickly).

Tip: Approach this exercise with a sense of fun and urgency. (Urgency because you are going to push yourself to skim as rapidly as possible).

Exercise 6

Set a very fast pace, using your finger or pen.

Words eliminated from the first section:

The, a, of. Often these three words can account for 10% o a document!

THE ADVENTURES OF SHERLOCK HOLMES

by

Sir Arthur Conan Doyle

A SCANDAL IN BOHEMIA

To Sherlock Holmes she is always x woman. I have seldom heard him mention her under any other name. In his eyes she eclipses and predominates x whole x her sex. It was not that he felt any emotion akin to love for Irene Adler. All emotions, and that one particularly, were abhorrent to his cold, precise but admirably balanced mind. He was, I take it, x most perfect reasoning and observing machine that x world has seen, but as x lover he would have placed himself in x false position. He never spoke x x softer passions, save with x gibe and x sneer. They were admirable things for x observer-- excellent for drawing x veil from men's motives and actions. But for x trained reasoner to admit such intrusions into his own delicate and finely adjusted temperament was to introduce x distracting factor which might throw x doubt upon all his mental results. Grit in x sensitive instrument, or x crack in one x his own high-power lenses, would not be more disturbing than x strong emotion in x nature such as his. And yet there was but one woman to him, and that woman was x late Irene Adler, x dubious and questionable memory.

I had seen little x Holmes lately. My marriage had drifted us away from each other. My own complete happiness, and x home-centered interests which rise up around x man who first finds himself master x his own establishment, were sufficient to absorb all my attention, while Holmes, who loathed every form x society with his whole Bohemian soul, remained in our lodgings in Baker Street, buried among his old books, and alternating from week to week between cocaine and ambition, x drowsiness x x drug, and x fierce energy x his own keen nature. He was still, as ever, deeply attracted by x study x crime, and occupied his immense faculties and extraordinary powers x observation in following out those clues, and clearing up those mysteries which had been abandoned as hopeless by x official police. From time to time I heard some vague account x his doings: x his summons to Odessa in x case x x Trepoff murder, x his clearing up x x singular tragedy x x Atkinson brothers at Trincomalee, and finally x x mission which he had accomplished so delicately and successfully for x reigning family x Holland. Beyond these signs x his activity, however, which I merely shared with all x readers x x daily press, I knew little x my former friend and companion.

One night--it was on x twentieth x March, 1888--I was returning from x journey to x patient (for I had now returned to civil practice), when my way led me through Baker Street. As I passed x well-remembered door, which must always be associated in my mind with my wooing, and with x dark incidents x x Study in Scarlet, I was seized with x keen desire to see Holmes again, and to know how he was employing his extraordinary powers. His rooms were brilliantly lit, and, even as I looked up, I saw his tall, spare figure pass twice in x dark silhouette against x blind. He was pacing x room swiftly, eagerly, with his head sunk upon his chest and his hands clasped behind him. To me, who knew his every mood and habit, his attitude and manner told their own story. He was at work again. He had risen out x his drug-created dreams and was hot upon x scent x some new problem. I rang x bell and was shown up to x chamber which had formerly been in part my own.

His manner was not effusive. It seldom was; but he was glad, I think, to see me. With hardly x word spoken, but with x kindly eye, he waved me to an armchair, threw across his case x cigars, and indicated x spirit case and x gasogene in x corner. Then he stood before x fire and looked me over in his singular introspective fashion.

"Wedlock suits you," he remarked. "I think, Watson, that you have put on seven and x half pounds since I saw you."

"Seven!" I answered.

"Indeed, I should have thought x little more. Just x trifle more, I fancy, Watson. And in practice again, I observe. You did not tell me that you intended to go into harness."

"Then, how do you know?"

"I see it, I deduce it. How do I know that you have been getting yourself very wet lately, and that you have x most clumsy and careless servant girl?"

"My dear Holmes," said I, "this is too much. You would certainly have been burned, had you lived x few centuries ago. It is true that I had x country walk on Thursday and came home in x dreadful mess, but as I have changed my clothes I can't imagine how you deduce it. As to Mary Jane, she is incorrigible, and my wife has given her notice, but there, again, I fail to see how you work it out."

He chuckled to himself and rubbed his long, nervous hands together.

"It is simplicity itself," said he; "my eyes tell me that on x inside x your left shoe, just where x firelight strikes it, x leather is scored by six almost parallel cuts. Obviously they have been caused by someone who has very carelessly scraped round x edges x x sole in order to remove crusted mud from it. Hence, you see, my double deduction that you had been out in vile weather, and that you had x particularly malignant boot-slitting specimen x x London slavey. As to your practice, if x gentleman walks into my rooms smelling x iodoform, with x black mark x nitrate x silver upon his right forefinger, and x bulge on x right side x his top-hat to show where he has secreted his stethoscope, I must be dull, indeed, if I do not pronounce him to be an active member x x medical profession."

I could not help laughing at x ease with which he explained his process x deduction. "When I hear you give your reasons," I remarked, "x thing always appears to me to be so ridiculously simple that I could easily do it myself, though at each successive instance x your reasoning I am baffled until you explain your process. And yet I believe that my eyes are as good as yours."

"Quite so," he answered, lighting x cigarette, and throwing himself down into an armchair. "You see, but you do not observe. X distinction is clear. For example, you have frequently seen x steps which lead up from x hall to this room."

"Frequently."

"How often?"

"Well, some hundreds x times."

"Then how many are there?"

"How many? I don't know."

"Quite so! You have not observed. And yet you have seen. That is just my point. Now, I know that there are seventeen steps, because I have both seen and observed. By-x-way, since you are interested in these little problems, and since you are good enough to chronicle one or two x my trifling experiences, you may be interested in this." He threw over x sheet x thick, pink-tinted note-paper which had been lying open upon x table. "It came by x last post," said he. "Read it aloud."

X note was undated, and without either signature or address.

"There will call upon you to-night, at x quarter to eight o'clock," it said, "x gentleman who desires to consult you upon x matter x x very deepest moment. Your recent services to one x x royal houses x Europe have shown that you are one who may safely be trusted with matters which are x an importance which can hardly be exaggerated. This account x you we have from all quarters received. Be in your chamber then at that hour, and do not take it amiss if your visitor wear x mask."

"This is indeed x mystery," I remarked. "What do you imagine that it means?"

"I have no data yet. It is x capital mistake to theorize before one has data. Insensibly one begins to twist facts to suit theories, instead x theories to suit facts. But x note itself. What do you deduce from it?"

I carefully examined x writing, and x paper upon which it was written.

"X man who wrote it was presumably well to do," I remarked, endeavoring to imitate my companion's processes. "Such paper could not be bought under half x crown x packet. It is peculiarly strong and stiff."

"Peculiar--that is x very word," said Holmes. "It is not an English paper at all. Hold it up to x light."

I did so, and saw x large "E" with x small "g," x "P," and x large "G" with x small "t" woven into x texture x x paper.

"What do you make x that?" asked Holmes.

"X name x x maker, no doubt; or his monogram, rather."

"Not at all. X 'G' with x small 't' stands for 'Gesellschaft,' which is x German for 'Company.' It is x customary contraction like our 'Co.' 'P,' x course, stands for 'Papier.' Now for x 'Eg.' Let us glance at our Continental Gazetteer." He took down x heavy brown volume from his shelves. "Eglow, Eglonitz--here we are, Egria. It is in x German-speaking country--in Bohemia, not far from Carlsbad. 'Remarkable as being x scene x x death x Wallenstein, and for its numerous glass-factories and paper-mills.' Ha, ha, my boy, what do you make x that?" His eyes sparkled, and he sent up x great blue triumphant cloud from his cigarette.

"X paper was made in Bohemia," I said.

"Precisely. And x man who wrote x note is x German. Do you note x peculiar construction x x sentence--'This account x you we have from all quarters received.' X Frenchman or Russian could not have written that. It is x German who is so uncourteous to his verbs. It only remains, therefore, to discover what is wanted by this German who writes upon Bohemian paper and prefers wearing x mask to showing his face. And here he comes, if I am not mistaken, to resolve all our doubts."

As he spoke there was x sharp sound x horses' hoofs and grating wheels against x curb, followed by x sharp pull at x bell. Holmes whistled.

"X pair, by x sound," said he. "Yes," he continued, glancing out x x window. "X nice little brougham and x pair x beauties. X hundred and fifty guineas apiece. There's money in this case, Watson, if there is nothing else."

"I think that I had better go, Holmes."

"Not x bit, Doctor. Stay where you are. I am lost without my Boswell. And this promises to be interesting. It would be x pity to miss it."

"But your client--"

"Never mind him. I may want your help, and so may he. Here he comes. Sit down in that armchair, Doctor, and give us your best attention."

X slow and heavy step, which had been heard upon x stairs and in x passage, paused immediately outside x door. Then there was x loud and authoritative tap.

"Come in!" said Holmes.

X man entered who could hardly have been less than six feet six inches in height, with x chest and limbs x x Hercules. His dress was rich with x richness which would, in England, be looked upon as akin to bad taste. Heavy bands x astrakhan were slashed across x sleeves and fronts x his double-breasted coat, while x deep blue cloak which was thrown over his shoulders was lined with flame-coloured silk and secured at x neck with x brooch which consisted x x single flaming beryl. Boots which extended halfway up his calves, and which were trimmed at x tops with rich brown fur, completed x impression x barbaric opulence which was suggested by his whole appearance. He carried x broad-brimmed hat in his hand, while he wore across x upper part x his face, extending down past x cheekbones, x black vizard mask, which he had apparently adjusted that very moment, for his hand was still raised to it as he entered. From x lower part x x face he appeared to be x man x strong character, with x thick, hanging lip, and x long, straight chin suggestive x resolution pushed to x length x obstinacy.

"You had my note?" he asked with x deep harsh voice and x strongly marked German accent. "I told you that I would call." He looked from one to x other x us, as if uncertain which to address.

"Pray take x seat," said Holmes. "This is my friend and colleague, Dr. Watson, who is occasionally good enough to help me in my cases. Whom have I x honor to address?"

"You may address me as x Count Von Kramm, x Bohemian nobleman. I understand that this gentleman, your friend, is x man x honor and discretion, whom I may trust with x matter x x most extreme importance. If not, I should much prefer to communicate with you alone."

I rose to go, but Holmes caught me by x wrist and pushed me back into my chair. "It is both, or none," said he. "You may say before this gentleman anything which you may say to me."

X Count shrugged his broad shoulders. "Then I must begin," said he, "by binding you both to absolute secrecy for two years; at x end x that time x matter will be x no importance. At present it is not too much to say that it is x such weight it may have an influence upon European history."

"I promise," said Holmes.
"And I."

Words eliminated from the next section:

The, a, of, to, in, is, you, it, he, was, for

Together these typically account for 20% of words

"X will excuse this mask," continued our strange visitor. "X august person who employs me wishes his agent x be unknown x x, and I may confess at once that x title by which I have just called myself x not exactly my own."

"I x aware x x," said Holmes dryly.

"X circumstances are x great delicacy, and every precaution has x be taken x quench what might grow x be an immense scandal and seriously compromise one x x reigning families x Europe. X speak plainly, x matter implicates x great House x Ormstein, hereditary kings x Bohemia."

"I x also aware x that," murmured Holmes, settling himself down x his armchair and closing his eyes.

Our visitor glanced with some apparent surprise at x languid, lounging figure x x man who had been no doubt depicted x him as x most incisive reasoner and most energetic agent x Europe. Holmes slowly reopened his eyes and looked impatiently at his gigantic client.

"If your Majesty would condescend x state your case," x remarked, "I should be better able x advise x."

X man sprang from his chair and paced up and down x room x uncontrollable agitation. Then, with x gesture x desperation, x tore x mask from his face and hurled x upon x ground. "X are right," x cried; "I am x King. Why should I attempt x conceal x?"

"Why, indeed?" murmured Holmes. "Your Majesty had not spoken before I x aware that I x addressing Wilhelm Gottsreich Sigismond von Ormstein, Grand Duke x Cassel-Felstein, and hereditary King x Bohemia."

"But x can understand," said our strange visitor, sitting down once more and passing his hand over his high white forehead, "x can understand that I am not accustomed x doing such business x my own person. Yet x matter x so delicate that I could not confide x x an agent without putting myself x his power. I have come incognito from Prague x x purpose x consulting x."

"Then, pray consult," said Holmes, shutting his eyes once more.

"X facts are briefly these: Some five years ago, during x lengthy visit x Warsaw, I made x acquaintance x x well-known adventuress, Irene Adler. X name x no doubt familiar x x."

"Kindly look her up x my index, Doctor," murmured Holmes without opening his eyes. X many years x had adopted x system x docketing all paragraphs concerning men and things, so that x x difficult x name x subject or x person on which x could not at once furnish information. X this case I found her biography sandwiched x between that x x Hebrew rabbi and that x x staff-commander who had written x monograph upon x deep-sea fishes.

"Let me see!" said Holmes. "Hum! Born x New Jersey x x year 1858. Contralto--hum! La Scala, hum! Prima donna Imperial Opera x Warsaw--yes! Retired from operatic stage--ha! Living x London--quite so! Your Majesty, as I understand, became entangled with this young person, wrote her some compromising letters, and x now desirous x getting those letters back."

"Precisely so. But how--"

"X there x secret marriage?"

"None."

"No legal papers or certificates?"

"None."

"Then I fail x follow your Majesty. If this young person should produce her letters x blackmailing or other purposes, how x she x prove their authenticity?"

"There x x writing."

"Pooh, pooh! Forgery."

"My private note-paper."

"Stolen."

"My own seal."

"Imitated."

"My photograph."

"Bought."

"We were both x x photograph."

"Oh, dear! That x very bad! Your Majesty has indeed committed an indiscretion."

"I x mad--insane."

"X have compromised yourself seriously."

"I x only Crown Prince then. I x young. I am but thirty now."

"X must be recovered."

"We have tried and failed."

"Your Majesty must pay. X must be bought."

"She will not sell."

"Stolen, then."

"Five attempts have been made. Twice burglars x my pay ransacked her house. Once we diverted her luggage when she traveled. Twice she has been waylaid. There has been no result."

"No sign x x?"

"Absolutely none."

Holmes laughed. "X x quite x pretty little problem," said x.

"But x very serious one x me," returned x King reproachfully.

"Very, indeed. And what does she propose x do with x photograph?"

"X ruin me."

"But how?"

"I am about x be married."

"So I have heard."

"X Clotilde Lothman von Saxe-Meningen, second daughter x x King x Scandinavia. X may know x strict principles x her family. She x herself x very soul x delicacy. X shadow x x doubt as x my conduct would bring x matter x an end."

"And Irene Adler?"

"Threatens x send them x photograph. And she will do x. I know that she will do x. X do not know her, but she has x soul x steel. She has x face x x most beautiful x women, and x mind x x most resolute x men. Rather than I should marry another woman, there are no lengths x which she would not go--none."

"X are sure that she has not sent x yet?"

"I am sure."

"And why?"

"Because she has said that she would send x on x day when x betrothal x publicly proclaimed. That will be next Monday."

"Oh, then we have three days yet," said Holmes with x yawn. "That x very fortunate, as I have one or two matters x importance x look into just at present. Your Majesty will, x course, stay x London x x present?"

"Certainly. X will find me at x Langham under x name x x Count Von Kramm."

"Then I shall drop x x line x let x know how we progress."

"Pray do so. I shall be all anxiety."

"Then, as x money?"

"X have carte blanche."

"Absolutely?"

"I tell x that I would give one x x provinces x my kingdom x have that photograph."

"And x present expenses?"

X King took x heavy chamois leather bag from under his cloak and laid x on x table.

"There are three hundred pounds x gold and seven hundred x notes," x said.

Holmes scribbled x receipt upon x sheet x his note-book and handed x x him.

"And Mademoiselle's address?" x asked.

"X Briony Lodge, Serpentine Avenue, St. John's Wood."

Holmes took x note x x. "One other question," said x. "X x photograph x cabinet?"

"X x."

"Then, good-night, your Majesty, and I trust that we shall soon have some good news x x. And good-night, Watson," x added, as x wheels x x royal brougham rolled down x street. "If x will be good enough x call x-morrow afternoon at three o'clock I should like x chat this little matter over with x."

Words eliminated from the next section:

The, a, of, to, in, is, you, it, he, was, for, on, are, as, his, they, I, at, be, have, had, by, what, all, were, we, your, can, said

Together these words typically account for 30% of words in a document. Almost a third of the document is eliminated and with practice you can read it easily...

II.

X three o'clock precisely X x x Baker Street, but Holmes x not yet returned. X landlady informed me that x x left x house shortly after eight o'clock x x morning. X sat down beside x fire, however, with x intention x awaiting him, however long x might x. X x already deeply interested x x inquiry, x, though x x surrounded x none x x grim and strange features which x associated with x two crimes which X x already recorded, still, x nature x x case and x exalted station x x client gave x x character x its own. Indeed, apart from x nature x x investigation which my friend x x hand, there x something x x masterly grasp x x situation, and x keen, incisive reasoning, which made x x pleasure x me x study x system x work, and x follow x quick, subtle methods x which x disentangled x most inextricable mysteries. So accustomed x X x x invariable success that x very possibility x x failing x ceased x enter into my head.

X x close upon four before x door opened, and x drunken-looking groom, ill-kempt and side-whiskered, with an inflamed face and disreputable clothes, walked into x room. Accustomed x X x x my friend's amazing powers x x use x disguises, X x x look three times before X x certain that x x indeed x. With x nod x vanished into x bedroom, whence x emerged x five minutes tweed-suited and respectable, x x old. Putting x hands into x pockets, x stretched out x legs x front x x fire and laughed heartily x some minutes.

"Well, really!" x cried, and then x choked and laughed again until x x obliged x lie back, limp and helpless, x x chair.

"X x x?"

"X's quite too funny. X am sure x could never guess how X employed my morning, or x X ended x doing."

"X x't imagine. X suppose that x x been watching x habits, and perhaps x house, x Miss Irene Adler."

"Quite so; but x sequel x rather unusual. X will tell x, however. X left x house x little after eight o'clock this morning x x character x x groom out x work. There x x wonderful sympathy and freemasonry among horsey men. X one x them, and x will know x that there x x know. X soon found Briony Lodge. X x x bijou villa, with x garden x x back, but built out x front right up x x road, two stories. Chubb lock x x door. Large sitting-room x x right side, well furnished, with long windows almost x x floor, and those preposterous English window fasteners which x child could open. Behind there x nothing remarkable, save that x passage window could x reached from x top x x coach-house. X walked round x and examined x closely from every point x view, but without noting anything else x interest.

"X then lounged down x street and found, x X expected, that there x x mews x x lane which runs down x one wall x x garden. X lent x ostlers x hand x rubbing down their horses, and received x exchange two pence, x glass x half and half, two fills x shag tobacco, and x much information x X could desire about Miss Adler, x say nothing x half x dozen other people x x neighborhood x whom X x not x x least interested, but whose biographies X x compelled x listen x."

"And x x Irene Adler?" X asked.

"Oh, she has turned x x men's heads down x that part. She x x daintiest thing under x bonnet x this planet. So say x Serpentine-mews, x x man. She lives quietly, sings x concerts, drives out x five every day, and returns x seven sharp x dinner. Seldom goes out x other times, except when she sings. Has only one male visitor, but x good deal x him. X x dark, handsome, and dashing, never calls less than once x day, and often twice. X x x Mr. Godfrey Norton, x x Inner Temple. See x advantages x x cabman x x confidant. X x driven him home x dozen times from Serpentine-mews, and knew x about him. When X x listened x x x x x tell, X began x walk up and down near Briony Lodge once more, and x think over my plan x campaign.

"This Godfrey Norton x evidently an important factor x x matter. X x x lawyer. That sounded ominous. X x x relation between them, and x x object x x repeated visits? X she x client, x friend, or x mistress? If x former, she x probably transferred x photograph x x keeping. If x latter, x x less likely. X issue x this question depended whether X should continue my work x Briony Lodge, or turn my attention x x gentleman's chambers x x Temple. X x x delicate point, and x widened x field x my inquiry. X fear that X bore x with these details, but X x x let x see my little difficulties, if x x x understand x situation."

"X am following x closely," X answered.

"X x still balancing x matter x my mind when x hansom cab drove up x Briony Lodge, and x gentleman sprang out. X x x remarkably handsome man, dark, aquiline, and moustached-- evidently x man x whom X x heard. X appeared x x x x great hurry, shouted x x cabman x wait, and brushed past x maid who opened x door with x air x x man who x thoroughly x home.

"X x x x house about half an hour, and X could catch glimpses x him x x windows x x sitting-room, pacing up and down, talking excitedly, and waving x arms. X her X could see nothing. Presently x emerged, looking even more flurried than before. X x stepped up x x cab, x pulled x gold watch from x pocket and looked x x earnestly, 'Drive like x devil,' x shouted, 'first x Gross & Hankey's x Regent Street, and then x x Church x St. Monica x x Edgeware Road. Half x guinea if x do x x twenty minutes!'

"Away x went, and X x just wondering whether X should not do well x follow them when up x lane came x neat little landau, x coachman with x coat only half-buttoned, and x tie under x ear, while x x tags x x harness x sticking out x x buckles. X hadn't pulled up before she shot out x x hall door and into x. X only caught x glimpse x her x x moment, but she x x lovely woman, with x face that x man might die x.

"'X Church x St. Monica, John,' she cried, 'and half x sovereign if x reach x x twenty minutes.'

"This x quite too good x lose, Watson. X x just balancing whether X should run x x, or whether X should perch behind her landau when x cab came through x street. X driver looked twice x such x shabby fare, but X jumped x before x could object. 'X Church x St. Monica,' x X, 'and half x sovereign if x reach x x twenty minutes.' X x twenty-five minutes x twelve, and x course x x clear enough x x x x wind.

"My cabby drove fast. X don't think X ever drove faster, but x others x there before us. X cab and x landau with their steaming horses x x front x x door when X arrived. X paid x man and hurried into x church. There x not x soul there save x two whom X x followed and x surpliced clergyman, who seemed x x expostulating with them. X x x three standing x x knot x front x x altar. X lounged up x side aisle like any other idler who has dropped into x church. Suddenly, x my surprise, x three x x altar faced round x me, and Godfrey Norton came running x hard x x could towards me.

"'Thank God,' x cried. 'X'll do. Come! Come!'

"'X then?' X asked.

"'Come, man, come, only three minutes, or x won't x legal.'

"X x half-dragged up x x altar, and before X knew where X x X found myself mumbling responses which x whispered x my ear, and vouching x things x which X knew nothing, and generally assisting x x secure tying up x Irene Adler, spinster, x Godfrey Norton, bachelor. X x x done x an instant, and there x x gentleman thanking me x x one side and x lady x x other, while x clergyman beamed x me x front. X x x most preposterous position x which X ever found myself x my life, and x x x thought x x that started me laughing just now. X seems that there x been some informality about their license, that x clergyman absolutely refused x marry them without x witness x some sort, and that my lucky appearance saved x bridegroom from having x sally out into x streets x search x x best man. X bride gave me x sovereign, and X mean x wear x x my watch-chain x memory x x occasion."

"This x x very unexpected turn x affairs," x X; "and x then?"

"Well, X found my plans very seriously menaced. X looked x if x pair might take an immediate departure, and so necessitate very prompt and energetic measures x my part. X x church door, however, x separated, x driving back x x Temple, and she x her own house. 'X shall drive out x x park x five x usual,' she x x she left him. X heard no more. X drove away x different directions, and X went off x make my own arrangements."

"Which x?"

"Some cold beef and x glass x beer," x answered, ringing x bell. "X x been too busy x think x food, and X am likely x x busier still this evening. X x way, Doctor, X shall want x co-operation."

"X shall x delighted."

"X don't mind breaking x law?"

"Not x x least."

"Nor running x chance x arrest?"

"Not x x good cause."

"Oh, x cause x excellent!"

"Then X am x man."

"X x sure that X might rely x x."

"But x x x x wish?"

"When Mrs. Turner has brought x x tray X will make x clear x x. Now," x x x x turned hungrily x x simple fare that our landlady x provided, "X must discuss x while X eat, x X x not much time. X x nearly five now. X two hours x must x x x scene x action. Miss Irene, or Madame, rather, returns from her drive x seven. X must x x Briony Lodge x meet her."

"And x then?"

"X must leave that x me. X x already arranged x x x occur. There x only one point x which X must insist. X must not interfere, come x may. X understand?"

"X am x x neutral?"

"X do nothing whatever. There will probably x some small unpleasantness. Do not join x x. X will end x my being conveyed into x house. Four or five minutes afterwards x sitting-room window will open. X x x station yourself close x that open window."

"Yes."

"X x x watch me, x X will x visible x x."

"Yes."

"And when X raise my hand--so--x will throw into x room x X give x x throw, and will, x x same time, raise x cry x fire. X quite follow me?"

"Entirely."

"X x nothing very formidable," x x, taking x long cigar- shaped roll from x pocket. "X x an ordinary plumber's smoke- rocket, fitted with x cap x either end x make x self-lighting. X task x confined x that. When x raise x cry x fire, x will x taken up x quite x number x people. X may then walk x x end x x street, and X will rejoin x x ten minutes. X hope that X x made myself clear?"

"X am x remain neutral, x get near x window, x watch x, and x x signal x throw x this object, then x raise x cry x fire, and x wait x x x corner x x street."

"Precisely."

"Then x may entirely rely x me."

"That x excellent. X think, perhaps, x x almost time that X prepare x x new role X x x play."

X disappeared into x bedroom and returned x x few minutes x x character x an amiable and simple-minded Nonconformist clergyman. X broad black hat, x baggy trousers, x white tie, x sympathetic smile, and general look x peering and benevolent curiosity x such x Mr. John Hare alone could x equaled. X x not merely that Holmes changed x costume. X expression, x manner, x very soul seemed x vary with every fresh part that x assumed. X stage lost x fine actor, even x science lost an acute reasoner, when x became x specialist x crime.

X x x quarter past six when x left Baker Street, and x still wanted ten minutes x x hour when x found ourselves x Serpentine Avenue. X x already dusk, and x lamps x just being lighted x x paced up and down x front x Briony Lodge, waiting x x coming x its occupant. X house x just such x X x pictured x from Sherlock Holmes' succinct description, but x locality appeared x x less private than X expected. X x contrary, x x small street x x quiet neighborhood, x x remarkably animated. There x x group x shabbily dressed men smoking and laughing x x corner, x scissors-grinder with x wheel, two guardsmen who x flirting with x nurse-girl, and several well-dressed young men who x lounging up and down with cigars x their mouths.

"X see," remarked Holmes, x x paced x and fro x front x x house, "this marriage rather simplifies matters. X photograph becomes x double-edged weapon now. X chances x that she would x x averse x its being seen x Mr. Godfrey Norton, x our client x x its coming x x eyes x x princess. Now x question x, Where x x x find x photograph?"

"Where, indeed?"

"X x most unlikely that she carries x about with her. X x cabinet size. Too large x easy concealment about x woman's dress. She knows that x King x capable x having her waylaid and searched. Two attempts x x sort x already been made. X may take x, then, that she does not carry x about with her."

"Where, then?"

"Her banker or her lawyer. There x that double possibility. But X am inclined x think neither. Women x naturally secretive, and x like x do their own secreting. Why should she hand x over x anyone else? She could trust her own guardianship, but she could not tell x indirect or political influence might x brought x bear upon x business man. Besides, remember that she x resolved x use x within x few days. X must x where she x lay her hands upon x. X must x x her own house."

"But x has twice been burgled."

"Pshaw! X did not know how x look."

"But how will x look?"

"X will not look."

"X then?"

"X will get her x show me."

"But she will refuse."

"She will not x able x. But X hear x rumble x wheels. X x her carriage. Now carry out my orders x x letter."

X x spoke x gleam x x side-lights x x carriage came round x curve x x avenue. X x x smart little landau which rattled up x x door x Briony Lodge. X x pulled up, one x x loafing men x x corner dashed forward x open x door x x hope x earning x copper, but x elbowed away x another loafer, who x rushed up with x same intention. X fierce quarrel broke out, which x increased x x two guardsmen, who took sides with one x x loungers, and x x scissors-grinder, who x equally hot upon x other side. X blow x struck, and x an instant x lady, who x stepped from her carriage, x x centre x x little knot x flushed and struggling men, who struck savagely x each other with their fists and sticks. Holmes dashed into x crowd x protect x lady; but just x x reached her x gave x cry and dropped x x ground, with x blood running freely down x face. X x fall x guardsmen took x their heels x one direction and x loungers x x other, while x number x better-dressed people, who x watched x scuffle without taking part x x, crowded x x help x lady and x attend x x injured man. Irene Adler, x X will still call her, x hurried up x steps; but she stood x x top with her superb figure outlined against x lights x x hall, looking back into x street.

"X x poor gentleman much hurt?" she asked.

"X x dead," cried several voices.

"No, no, there's life x him!" shouted another. "But x'll x gone before x x get him x hospital."

"X's x brave fellow," x woman. "X would x x x lady's purse and watch if x hadn't been x him. X x x gang, and x rough one, too. Ah, x's breathing now."

"X x't lie x x street. May x bring him x, marm?"

"Surely. Bring him into x sitting-room. There x x comfortable sofa. This way, please!"

Slowly and solemnly x x borne into Briony Lodge and laid out x x principal room, while X still observed x proceedings from my post x x window. X lamps x been lit, but x blinds x not been drawn, so that X could see Holmes x x lay upon x couch. X do not know whether x x seized with compunction x that moment x x part x x playing, but X know that X never felt more heartily ashamed x myself x my life than when X saw x beautiful creature against whom X x conspiring, or x grace and kindliness with which she waited upon x injured man. And yet x would x x blackest treachery x Holmes x draw back now from x part which x x intrusted x me. X hardened my heart, and took x smoke-rocket from under my ulster. After x, X thought, x x not injuring her. X x but preventing her from injuring another.

Holmes x sat up upon x couch, and X saw him motion like x man who x x need x air. X maid rushed across and threw open x window. X x same instant X saw him raise x hand and x x signal X tossed my rocket into x room with x cry x "Fire!" X word x no sooner out x my mouth than x whole crowd x spectators, well dressed and ill--gentlemen, ostlers, and servant-maids--joined x x general shriek x "Fire!" Thick clouds x smoke curled through x room and out x x open window. X caught x glimpse x rushing figures, and x moment later x voice x Holmes from within assuring them that x x x false alarm. Slipping through x shouting crowd X made my way x x corner x x street, and x ten minutes x rejoiced x find my friend's arm x mine, and x get away from x scene x uproar. X walked swiftly and x silence x some few minutes until x x turned down one x x quiet streets which lead towards x Edgeware Road.

"X did x very nicely, Doctor," x remarked. "Nothing could x been better. X x x right."

"X x x photograph?"

"X know where x x."

"And how did x find out?"

"She showed me, x X told x she would."

"X am still x x dark."

"X do not wish x make x mystery," x x, laughing. "X matter x perfectly simple. X, x course, saw that everyone x x street x an accomplice. X x x engaged x x evening."

"X guessed x much."

"Then, when x row broke out, X x x little moist red paint x x palm x my hand. X rushed forward, fell down, clapped my hand x my face, and became x piteous spectacle. X x an old trick."

"That also X could fathom."

"Then x carried me x. She x bound x x me x. X else could she do? And into her sitting-room, which x x very room which X suspected. X lay between that and her bedroom, and X x determined x see which. X laid me x x couch, X motioned x air, x x compelled x open x window, and x x x chance."

"How did that help x?"

"X x x-important. When x woman thinks that her house x x fire, her instinct x x once x rush x x thing which she values most. X x x perfectly overpowering impulse, and X x more than once taken advantage x x. X x case x x Darlington substitution scandal x x x use x me, and also x x Arnsworth Castle business. X married woman grabs x her baby; an unmarried one reaches x her jewel-box. Now x x clear x me that our lady x x-day x nothing x x house more precious x her than x x x x quest x. She would rush x secure x. X alarm x fire x admirably done. X smoke and shouting x enough x shake nerves x steel. She responded beautifully. X photograph x x x recess behind x sliding panel just above x right bell-pull. She x there x an instant, and X caught x glimpse x x x she half-drew x out. When X cried out that x x x false alarm, she replaced x, glanced x x rocket, rushed from x room, and X x not seen her since. X rose, and, making my excuses, escaped from x house. X hesitated whether x attempt x secure x photograph x once; but x coachman x come x, and x x x watching me narrowly x seemed safer x wait. X little over-precipitance may ruin x."

"And now?" X asked.

"Our quest x practically finished. X shall call with x King x-morrow, and with x, if x care x come with us. X will x shown into x sitting-room x wait x x lady, but x x probable that when she comes she may find neither us nor x photograph. X might x x satisfaction x x Majesty x regain x with x own hands."

"And when will x call?"

"X eight x x morning. She will not x up, so that x shall x x clear field. Besides, x must x prompt, x this marriage may mean x complete change x her life and habits. X must wire x x King without delay."

X x reached Baker Street and x stopped x x door. X x searching x pockets x x key when someone passing x:

"Good-night, Mister Sherlock Holmes."

There x several people x x pavement x x time, but x greeting appeared x come from x slim youth x an ulster who x hurried x.

"X've heard that voice before," x Holmes, staring down x dimly lit street. "Now, X wonder who x deuce that could x been."

Words eliminated from the next section:

The, a, of, to, in, is, you, it, he, was, for, on, are, as, with, his, they, I, at, be, this, have, from, had, by, what, all, were, we, when, your, can, said, an, each, which, she, do, how, their, will, up, other, about, out, many, then, them, these, so, her, would, him, into, has, more, see, number, way, could, people, water, been, call, who, its, now, long, down, day, did, may

Together these words typically account for 45% of words in a document. Working at these levels of elimination is a skill that needs much practice. The function of this exercise is to show you that reading *all* the words is often unnecessary.

III.

X slept x Baker Street x night, x x x engaged upon our toast x coffee x x morning x x King x Bohemia rushed x x room.

"X x really got x!" x cried, grasping Sherlock Holmes x either shoulder x looking eagerly x x face.

"Not yet."

"But x x hopes?"

"X x hopes."

"X, come. X am x impatience x x gone."

"X must x x cab."

"No, my brougham x waiting."

"X x x simplify matters." X descended x started off once x x Briony Lodge.

"Irene Adler x married," remarked Holmes.

"Married! X?"

"Yesterday."

"But x whom?"

"X x English lawyer named Norton."

"But x x not love x."

"X am x hopes x x does."

"X why x hopes?"

"Because x x spare x Majesty x fear x future annoyance. If x lady loves x husband, x does not love x Majesty. If x does not love x Majesty, there x no reason why x should interfere x x Majesty's plan."

"X x true. X yet--Well! X wish x x x x my own station! X x queen x x x made!" X relapsed x x moody silence, x x not broken until x drew x x Serpentine Avenue.

X door x Briony Lodge x open, x x elderly woman stood upon x steps. X watched us x x sardonic eye x x stepped x x brougham.

"Mr. Sherlock Holmes, X believe?" x x.

"X am Mr. Holmes," answered my companion, looking x x x x questioning x rather startled gaze.

"Indeed! My mistress told me x x x likely x x. X left x morning x x husband x x 5:15 train x Charing Cross x x Continent."

"X!" Sherlock Holmes staggered back, white x chagrin x surprise. "X x mean x x x left England?"

"Never x return."

"X x papers?" asked x King hoarsely. "X x lost."

"X shall x." X pushed past x servant x rushed x x drawing-room, followed x x King x myself. X furniture x scattered x x every direction, x dismantled shelves x open drawers, x if x lady x hurriedly ransacked x before x flight. Holmes rushed x x bell-pull, tore back x small sliding shutter, x, plunging x x hand, pulled x x photograph x x letter. X photograph x x Irene Adler herself x evening dress, x letter x super-scribed x "Sherlock Holmes, Esq. X x left till called x." My friend tore x open x x x three read x together. X x dated x midnight x x preceding night x ran x x x:

"MY DEAR MR. SHERLOCK HOLMES,--
X really x x very well. X took me x completely. Until after x alarm x fire, X x not x suspicion. But x, x X found x X x betrayed myself, X began x think. X x x warned against x months ago. X x x told x if x King employed x agent x x certainly x x. X x address x x given me. Yet, x x x, x made me reveal x x wanted x know. Even after X became suspicious, X found x hard x think evil x such x dear, kind old clergyman. But, x know, X x x trained x x actress myself. Male costume x nothing new x me. X often take advantage x x freedom x x gives. X sent John, x coachman, x watch x, ran x stairs, got x my walking-clothes, x X x x, x came x just x x departed.

"Well, X followed x x x door, x x made sure x X x really x object x interest x x celebrated Mr. Sherlock Holmes. X X, rather imprudently, wished x good-night, x started x x Temple x x my husband.

"X both thought x best resource x flight, x pursued x x formidable x antagonist; x x x find x nest empty x x x x-morrow. X x x photograph, x client x rest x peace. X love x am loved x x better man than x. X King x x x x x without hindrance x one whom x x cruelly wronged. X keep x only x safeguard myself, x x preserve x weapon x x always secure me x any steps x x might take x x future. X leave x photograph x x might care x possess; x X remain, dear Mr. Sherlock Holmes,

"Very truly yours,
"IRENE NORTON, née ADLER."

"X x woman--oh, x x woman!" cried x King x Bohemia, x x x x three read x epistle. "X X not tell x x quick x resolute x x? X x not x made x admirable queen? X x not x pity x x x not x my level?"

"X x X x seen x x lady x seems indeed x x x x very different level x x Majesty," x Holmes coldly. "X am sorry x X x not x able x bring x Majesty's business x x x successful conclusion."

"X x contrary, my dear sir," cried x King; "nothing x x x successful. X know x x word x inviolate. X photograph x x x safe x if x x x x fire."

"X am glad x hear x Majesty say x."

"X am immensely indebted x x. Pray tell me x x x X x reward x. X ring--" X slipped x emerald snake ring x x finger x held x x upon x palm x x hand.

"X Majesty x something x X should value even x highly," x Holmes.

"X x but x name x."

"X photograph!"

X King stared x x x amazement.

"Irene's photograph!" x cried. "Certainly, if x wish x."

"X thank x Majesty. X there x no x x x done x x matter. X x x honor x wish x x very good-morning." X bowed, x, turning away without observing x hand x x King x stretched x x x, x set off x my company x x chambers.

X x x x x great scandal threatened x affect x kingdom x Bohemia, x x x best plans x Mr. Sherlock Holmes x beaten x x woman's wit. X used x make merry over x cleverness x women, but X x not heard x x x x late. X x x speaks x Irene Adler, or x x refers x x photograph, x x always under x honorable title x x woman.

The End.

"I heard his library burned down and both books were destroyed --- and one of them hadn't even been colored in yet."
John Dawkins

Part IV

Using Speed Reading as a Study Technique

Many people learn to speed read in order to study or understand documents much more quickly.

However, there is more to effective study than simply reading quickly. This section brings you through study techniques of proven benefit.

Chapter 11

Speed Reading and Study

Most students under-perform, not because of lack of effort or talent, but because of lack of purpose and structure to their studying. This chapter gives an overview of how to structure a reading session when you are studying.

A student who can read rapidly, confidently and with good retention has an enormous advantage. He or she should excel. When good reading techniques are learnt and implemented most students can improve their grades while spending less time studying. (Obviously, the benefits may be greater in History or Medicine than in Mathematics).

"Today a reader, tomorrow a leader."

W. Fusselman

Many students often just sit down with their textbooks and start reading. (If this sounds like you be happy! This is such an inefficient way to study that it will be very easy to improve). This is similar to wanting to walk from A to B and simply standing up and walking. You'd never do that. You'd first check how far it is, consult the maps, check the best direction to take. You'd figure out how long it would take to get there, the best route, etc., etc.

So it is with studying. Good planning pays rich dividends. You should have an overview of your year's study; this semester's study; a close idea of what you will be studying this week; know what you want to accomplish this evening and an *exact* idea of what you will study for the next half hour and what you want to get out of it.

There are several good ways to study. If you are already using a well-established, researched technique to good effect then you should continue with it. Otherwise, use this seven-step technique for each study session.

1. Prepare
2. Motivation
3. Preview
4. Overview
5. Read
6. Review
7. Revise

"Passive study is no study at all"
Professor Mc Gonnagal

Prepare

Set aside the time and place. It should go without saying that people study best in a quiet place where they will not be disturbed. However, lots of people seem to set themselves up for distraction. Don't do it. It seems many of us set up situations where we'll be distracted so that we'll have an excuse not to study, etc. Don't do it! If you dislike study resolve to do it much more effectively so you can get by with less of it and still achieve your goals.

Have a clear desk except for the books and equipment you'll need. Even if you are using on your computer to study you will still need a pen and your notebook to take notes, make comments, etc.

Switch your mobile phone completely off.

Be aware of your posture. Take a couple of deep breaths in and exhale slowly to the count of 10.

Music

The function of music whilst studying is:

* To drown out sound distractions
* To calm the body and make the mind more receptive
* To make the overall learning experience more enjoyable

It is NOT to enjoy the music for itself or to sing along to.

The best music seems to be orchestral music from the Baroque era. This may not be your cup of tea ... so what, you are here to study effectively and enjoyably. This will help and after five minutes you will not hear it as it plays in the background. There are a number of studies showing that this type of music can help concentration, memory and recall. Playing some Mozart in the background has even been shown to increase someone's I.Q.!

Any music that has vocals is generally unsuitable, especially if it is in your native language. The words demand attention and confuse the brain from its main task. Any music that has a rapid beat accelerates your body's rhythm and makes it more difficult to study.

Time

You need to set aside the time to study. Study is best broken down into chunks lasting no more than 20-30 minutes. A *brief* break and stretch is then needed before continuing, (this should only last a minute or two). Every hour you should take a five minute break and every 2 hours a longer break. Just as you wouldn't walk all day without food you shouldn't study without structured, *planned* breaks. Without the breaks the study becomes less effective as concentration wanes, fatigue sets in.and minds wander. The research in the area shows that the 20-30 minute time period of study is optimal for most people.

"The mere brute pleasure of reading ---the sort of
pleasure a cow must
have in grazing."
Gilbert K. Chesterton

Motivation

Without a clear goal your study will be unfocused and rambling. You need to state very clearly what it is you want to achieve and how you are going to achieve it. For instance, "I want to study chapter 5, to be able to write down the main events, how the theme developed and any changes in style". It is always best to write down these goals. Since this is only for yourself a few squiggles or shorthand is usually enough. For the above I would have written "ch 5, ev, th, sty".

The goal must be realistic. You should set a challenging but attainable goal. There is no point in attempting to memorise a whole encyclopaedia in a half-hour. Set your goal and reach it... be stubborn. It is important to reach your objective most times. If you are not, try being more realistic when goal setting and resolve firmly to achieve them.

Imagine yourself happy and smiling when you accomplish the goal in a half-hour. If you are religious, say a brief prayer that you will be helped and guided in the next half-hour. Briefly remember why you are studying. Even if you don't like the subject, but have to do it, remember to do it quickly and well -so that you'll be free all the sooner!

It is important that you set a good pace for yourself. If you are lolling around you won't achieve much.

Preview-Overview-Read-Review

Now the proper study really begins. By following the cycle of Preview-Overview-Read-Review you will remember much more than if you just read the material.

Preview

Quickly go through what you want to study. See how many pages there are. Read the headings, look at the pictures, if there is an introduction or summary read it.

"To read without reflecting is like eating without digesting."

Edmund Burke

Overview

If it is printed material be sure to use your finger or pen to pace your reading. Read at 2-3 times your baseline speed. Just aim to pick up the major points. (Refer back to Part III for a discussion on overview and skimming skills).

Read

You now should have a good idea of what you are studying and how it is structured. Next you should read to fully understand and maximise what you remember. It is VERY important to have your pen and notepad handy. Remember: "Passive study is no study". Here you need to be constantly underlining, jotting things down, etc. There is no need to write long, grammatically correct notes. Simple reminders of what you need to remember should be sufficient.

If you are reading a printed book, mark it, underline it ... this helps lock things into your memory and makes revision quicker. If you are worried about defacing the book mark it in pencil.

Keep the pace up, and make lots of mini-notes and under-linings. For difficult material it is sometimes necessary to reread several times. That's ok, try and plan for that beforehand though. Typically people should plan to spend about 15 minutes in this reading stage. The rest of the study period is spent in the other stages. (Overall, this system saves a lot of time and make for more effective study).

"I hear and I forget; I see and I remember; I write and I understand."

-- Chinese Proverb

Review

At this stage you should be able to make a good summary of what you have studied. You should spend 5 minutes writing down the main points that you remember. Make a mental note of what needs to be double-checked in the last rapid re-read. (When writing down the summary there is no need to write full sentences. That's not time-efficient. But it is necessary to write down the **key** words as this solidifies it in your memory).

Now, rapidly go through the material again, at 2-3 times normal speed. Making a note of important things that you forgot.

Give yourself a pat on the back. This study period is over. Smile and take the planned break.

Revision

Memory is a peculiar thing! Mostly it fades with time. If you read an article or attended a lecture six months ago and almost remember nothing from it what was the point of being there? And yet this is what generally happens. We attend a class or do some study, leave it and go on to study the next thing. Why bother? If you do not revise the time spent studying will have been mostly wasted. Yet a small and periodic revision is all that is required to keep what you learnt alive.

The graph below illustrates the typical memory loss with no revision.

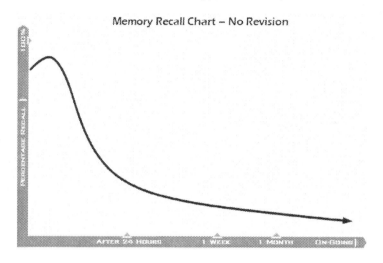

Note the huge memory loss after just 24 hours. Even this erodes further over time until, after six months, little remains. But do not despair, just a little planning and time will keep your memory topped up.

If the original study session was 20 minutes these can be squeezed down into as little as 5 minutes. Glance through your notes; read it at rapid speed; then jot down, in shorthand, the main points.

Repeat this after one day, one week, one month and six months. This way you can recall nearly everything.

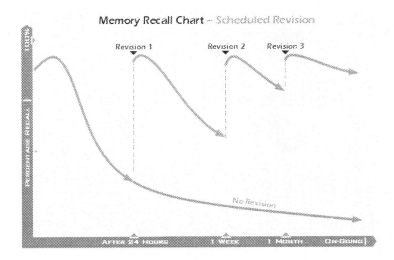

Memory Recall Chart – Scheduled Revision

Be sure to include your periodic revision in your overall study plan for the year.

(This chapter has dealt with just a few aspects of study and memory. If you are a student your ability to learn quickly and effectively is your most vital tool. It can always be improved upon. There are some excellent books dedicated solely to study. We recommend one by Tony Buzan).

Part V

Wrap-up

Last words of advice...

Making the improvements in
your reading permanent.

Chapter 12

Consolidating your gains in reading speed

A few closing remarks about how to ensure you become a fast, effective reader for life.

"Use it or lose it"

For many people just doing the course will be enough for them to permanently break bad habits. They achieve a step improvement in their reading and never go back.

However, as these bad habits have often been reinforced by years of slow reading there is a strong tendency for them to reassert themselves. To prevent this you should aim to do a speed session once a week. Set aside 10-15 minutes. Aim to do it at the same time and place every week. For me it is Tuesday mornings when I start work, before checking my emails.

Even if you are a good reader without bad habits you should do a weekly practise session. The old adage "Use it or lose it" applies. Unless you push yourself occasionally there will be a tendency to slip back into slower, less efficient reading.

Varying your reading speed

Just because you can speed-read doesn't mean that you always should. Religious or philosophical works are often meant to be pondered and mulled over. Reading them quickly might get you good marks in Sunday School but you might be missing the point.

When reading simply for pleasure read at whatever pace gives you the most pleasure. It is important to note that good, proficient readers tend to enjoy books the most. If it takes you a week or two to read a book you might have forgotten lots before the plot even twists. You wouldn't drag a movie out over weeks. Novels are the same ... if you can comfortably read them at a good pace it is so easy to become engrossed in the book.

When reading for work. It is usually best to be efficient, get the job done and move on. Quite often it is sufficient to skim through documents and reread the important sections. In these cases you should treat it as study. (See Part IV).

Congratulations! You should now be an honours graduate of the ReadPal Speed Reading School.

After you have finished the ReadPal Speed course you should complete the following:

My reading speed is now .... (well done!).

I undertake to:

☐ Maintain this by using a pacer, (pen or finger), as much as possible over the next .... weeks.

☐ Maintain and improve upon this speed by practising speed reading ...... times a week for ...... weeks.

It is a great motivator to calculate how many hours you spend reading every year and how much time you will save if you continue reading at your new improved rate. (Hours saved equals ....)

Signed ....

Last Word

ReadPal will be brining out further versions of this book in the future. If you feel we can improve on it please let us know by emailing us, (details are on our site, www.readpal.com). Your comments are much appreciated. Also please tell your friends about ReadPal... it can help them too!

Visit our website regularly to download free books, find reading links, software and other speed reading products. We are constantly updating and making more material available to you.

Lastly, I hope YOU enjoyed and benefited from the course. Thank you, from myself, Louis, and all at ReadPal.

Dr Louis Crowe.

"Book lovers never go to bed alone".
Anonymous

Appendix 1
Progress Chart

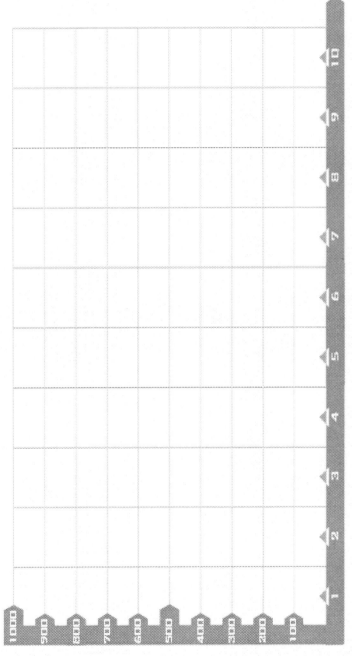

Printed in the United States
52042LVS00002B